# A Student's Companion to Hacker Handbooks

**Second Edition**

**Contributing Authors**

Sylvia Basile
*Midlands Technical College*

Sandra Chumchal
*Blinn College*

Sarah Gottschall
*Prince George's Community College*

Paul Madachy
*Prince George's Community College*

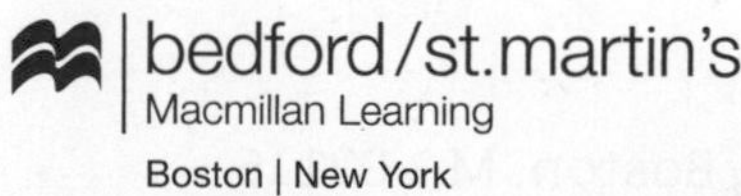
bedford/st.martin's
Macmillan Learning
Boston | New York

Library of Congress Control Number: 2020936831

ISBN 978-1-319-24421-7

Printed in the United States of America.
5 6 25 24 23

***Acknowledgments***
James J. Bernstein and Joseph Bernstein, "Texting at the Light and Other Forms of Device Distraction behind the Wheel," *BMC Public Health* 15 (2015), 968; doi: 10.1186/s12889-015-2343-8. (Accessed from https://www.ncbi.nlm.nih.gov/pmc/articles/PMC4584002.) Copyright © 2015 James J. Bernstein and Joseph Bernstein. This article is distributed under the terms of the Creative Commons Attribution 4.0 International License: http://creativecommons.org/licenses/by/4.0/.

Debra Kahn, "Melting Ice Could Cause More California Droughts," *E&E News*, December 5, 2017, https://www.eenews.net/stories/1060068087/. Copyright © 2017. Reprinted by permission.

*For information, write:* Bedford/St. Martin's, 75 Arlington Street, Boston, MA 02116

# A Note for Instructors

The information, activities, tools, and exercises in this workbook offer developing college writers help with and practice in key writing, research, and grammar skills. *A Student's Companion to Hacker Handbooks* can be used to give students in paired, co-requisite, or "ALP" sections of composition success-building extra practice with a variety of topics. The exercises in the workbook can be used in a variety of ways:

- homework
- classroom practice
- quizzes
- individualized self-teaching assignments
- writing center or learning lab worksheets

If you have adopted a Hacker/Sommers handbook for your course, you may want to consult the chart on the inside back cover, which correlates the content in this workbook with the coverage in the handbooks — *Rules for Writers*, *A Writer's Reference*, *A Pocket Style Manual*, *The Bedford Handbook*, and *Writer's Help*.

The workbook is organized in four parts. **Part 1** covers the transition from high school writing to college writing and includes important strategies for college success, such as managing your time and using academic etiquette. **Part 2** discusses topics common to first-year composition courses: essay and paragraph development, active reading, audience awareness, peer review, revision, and working with sources. Each of the chapters includes brief reflective activities. **Part 3** contains exercises in a variety of rhetorical and research skills, such as using topic sentences, avoiding plagiarism, and reading critically. **Part 4** includes exercises in sentence-level topics: parallelism, subject-verb agreement, fragments, commas and quotation marks, and more.

Exercises and activities are spaced so that students can complete their work in this workbook. Answers for most of the exercises in Parts 3 and 4 are included in the back of this book for convenience.

This workbook is available for student purchase in print and digital options.

- *A Student's Companion to Hacker Handbooks* (stand-alone): ISBN 978-1-319-24421-7.
- *A Student's Companion to Hacker Handbooks* packaged with a Hacker/Sommers handbook, available at a significant discount. Contact your Macmillan Learning sales representative.
- *A Student's Companion to Hacker Handbooks* Vital Source e-book. Contact your Macmillan Learning sales representative.

And of course we at Bedford/St. Martin's are available for you — whether you are new to our print and media products, new to this course, or in need of new ideas. Contact your sales representative to find out how we can help.

**Contributors and reviewers** We were grateful to have help from several contributing authors, all expert teachers of writing: Sylvia Basile (Midlands Technical College) wrote a chapter on integrating sources; Sandra Chumchal (Blinn College) contributed both a chapter and activities on reading skills; Sarah Gottschall (Prince George's Community College) wrote plagiarism and thesis exercises; and Paul Madachy (Prince George's Community College) contributed a chapter on audience. In addition, we were lucky to learn from excellent reviewers who helped us shape the content of *A Student's Companion to Hacker Handbooks*: Lindsay Brand, St. Charles Community College; Cathy J. Clements, State Fair Community College; Jerome Cusson, University of Memphis; Robert Perry Ivey, Gordon State College; Katherine Fredlund, University of Memphis; Jeffrey Miller, St. Charles Community College; Cecilia Nina Myers, University of Memphis; Jayme Novara, St. Charles Community College; Patricia Pallis, Naugatuck Valley Community College; Kevin Sanders, University of Arkansas, Pine Bluff; Ellen Shur, Middlesex County College; James R. Sodon, St. Louis Community College, Florissant Valley; Jessica Swan, University of Memphis; Jeana West, Murray State College.

# Contents

## PART 3 *Practicing Reading, Writing, and Research Skills* 147

**PART 1**
*Succeeding in College*

## CHAPTER 1

# Becoming a college writer

Think for a minute about your high school writing experiences—perhaps you wrote an analysis of *The Adventures of Huckleberry Finn*, one or more lab reports for biology, a response to a film about Afghanistan, or a poem about growing up. You may find not only that more writing is expected when you get to college, but also that more is expected of you as a writer. Sometimes you'll wonder why no one is telling you what the "more" is, or exactly how college writing differs from high school writing.

What's certain is that you will be required to write in almost all of your college courses—even if you major in fields such as engineering, nursing, or business. Developing different attitudes toward and approaches to academic writing can help you to become a successful writer in all of your college courses.

## 1a Be open-minded about the "rules" of good writing

Think for a moment about all the rules of good writing that you learned throughout elementary, middle, and high school. Which rules have really stuck in your mind? Which ones do you follow without question?

**WRITING ACTIVITY** ✦ Take a few minutes to write down four or five rules about writing that you have learned in your past school experiences. Did you find these rules useful? Paralyzing? Confusing? Clear?

**The five-paragraph essay** In the previous writing activity, you may have talked about the five-paragraph essay, a form of writing taught in many middle schools and high schools in the United States. It requires an introduction, three body paragraphs, and a conclusion. It was probably a useful formula for you as you composed in-class essays and essays for standardized tests. But the kind of writing you will be asked to do in college may be more complex or just less predictable; the form may not continue to work for you in every writing situation. Be open to writing longer essays and using different types of organization. Be open to composing a hybrid of paragraphs and visuals. Be open to writing that is not restricted to reporting information or giving a personal response; many college assignments ask you to combine those purposes with other purposes, such as analyzing and arguing.

**Using first person (*I* or *we*)** A lot of high school writing is awkward to read because of rules related to the point of view of an essay. In college, you will need to learn about your professors' expectations, but be open to the idea that for some writing, the use of *I* and *we* may in fact be encouraged. College professors may expect you to write with a more personal voice, rather than using stale sentences such as, "One might argue that one has the right to free speech in social media posts. . . ." You may also be expected to report field research experiences or steps in other research with *I* or *we*. You will find that some college professors have strong feelings about this topic, so it's a good idea to ask before a draft is due.

**Collaborating with other writers and thinkers** You may have had an experience in which a teacher questioned a written response that sounded too much like a classmate's or specifically prohibited working on writing assignments with others in the class. College professors in a first-year course expect you to do your own writing and to cite sources when you borrow language or ideas from another writer, but they also want to prepare you for courses and workplace tasks in which collaboration will be expected. You will find that college assignments often require collaboration and encourage you to seek feedback. Teachers will expect you to approach academic writing tasks as a participant in a world of ideas rather than as a reporter of others' ideas. You can think of research writing as collaborating, in a sense, with other thinkers in order to answer a research question. You will be expected to cite published sources, of course, but casual conversations you have with classmates, writing center staff, peers, and others can inform your thinking about a subject you will write about.

##  1b Adopt good habits of mind

College writing gives you the opportunity to develop skills, such as supporting arguments with evidence, writing effective thesis statements, and using transitions well, but it also gives you the opportunity to develop habits. Successful college students develop certain "habits of mind," a way of approaching learning that leads to success.

In 2011, the Council of Writing Program Administrators (CWPA), the National Council of Teachers of English (NCTE), and the National Writing Project (NWP) identified eight habits of mind that successful college students adopt. The following overview is adapted from the three organizations' report titled "Framework for Success in Postsecondary Writing."

*Curiosity.* Are you the kind of person who always wants to know more? This habit of mind will serve you well in courses in which your curiosity about issues, problems, people, or policies can form the backbone of a writing project.

**WRITING ACTIVITY** ✦ What are you most curious to learn about? What experiences have you had in which your curiosity has led you to an interesting discovery or to more questions?

*Openness.* Some people are more open than others to new ideas and experiences and new ways of thinking about the world. Being open to other perspectives and positions can help you to frame sound arguments and counterarguments and solve other college writing challenges in thoughtful ways.

**WRITING ACTIVITY** ✦ In the family or part of the world in which you grew up, did people tend to be very open, not open at all, or somewhere in the middle? Thinking about your own level of open-mindedness, reflect on how much or how little your own attitude toward a quality like openness is a result of the attitudes of the people around you.

*Engagement.* Successful college writers are involved in their own learning process. Students who are engaged put effort into their classes, knowing that they'll get something out of their classes—something other than a grade. They participate in their own learning by planning, seeking feedback when they need to, and communicating with peers and professors to create their own success.

**WRITING ACTIVITY** ✦ Write about a few of the ways you try (or plan to try) to be involved in your own learning. What does engagement look like to you?

*Creativity.* You may think that you have to be an artist, poet, or musician to display creativity. This is not the case. Scientists use creativity every day in coming up with ways to investigate questions in their field. Engineers and technicians approach problem-solving in creative ways. Retail managers use creativity in displaying merchandise and motivating employees.

**WRITING ACTIVITY** ✦ Think about the field you plan to enter. What forms might creativity take in that field?

*Persistence.* You are probably used to juggling long-term and short-term commitments—both in school and in your everyday life. Paying attention to your commitments and being persistent enough to see them through, even when the commitments are challenging, are good indicators that you will be successful in college.

**WRITING ACTIVITY** ✦ Describe a time when you faced and overcame an obstacle in an academic setting. What did you learn from that experience?

*Responsibility.* College will require you to be responsible in ways you may not have had to be before. Two responsibilities you will face as an academic writer are to represent the ideas of others fairly and to give credit to writers whose ideas and language you borrow for your own purposes.

**WRITING ACTIVITY** ✦ Why do you think academic responsibility is important? What kind of experience have you had already with this kind of responsibility?

*Flexibility.* Would your friends say that you are the kind of person who can "go with the flow"? Do you adapt easily to changing situations? If so, you will find college easier, especially college writing. When you find, for example, that you've written a draft that doesn't address the right audience or that your peer review group doesn't understand at all, you will be able to adapt. Being flexible enough to adapt to the demands of different writing projects is an important habit of mind.

**WRITING ACTIVITY** ✦ Describe a situation in which you've had to make changes based on a situation you couldn't control. Did you do so easily or with difficulty?

---

---

---

*Metacognition (reflection).* As a learner, you have probably been asked to think back on a learning experience and comment on what went well or not well, what you learned or wish you had learned, or what decisions you made or didn't make. Writers who reflect on their own processes and decisions are better able to transfer writing skills to future assignments.

**WRITING ACTIVITY** ✦ Reflect on your many experiences as a writer. What was your most satisfying experience as a writer? What made it so?

---

---

---

---

---

# CHAPTER 2
# Building your confidence

Confidence is a positive and realistic belief about yourself and your talents and traits. Words like *assertive*, *poised*, *optimistic*, *eager*, *proud*, and *mature* are often seen as synonymous with *confident*. Confidence can help drive and shape your experiences as a student, performer, athlete, employee, parent, and the many other roles you play in your life. Conversely, a lack of confidence can result in a poor performance in those same roles.

Here are some important reasons to develop confidence:

- **Confidence helps sell who you are.** Knowledge, skills, and experience are necessary and important. If you do not possess and project confidence, others may not realize you have these qualities.
- **Confidence reassures others.** It can create trust in the people in your life, whether they are your peers, classmates, coworkers, or loved ones.

This chapter explores the role that confidence plays in everyday success and offers strategies on building your confidence for all of the roles you play in your life.

## 2a Grow your level of confidence

Have you had any trouble maintaining your confidence since you started college? It may surprise you to learn that you are not the only first-year student who feels this way. Many new college students feel just like you do: not very certain of all that lies ahead and unsure about how to deal with a number of challenges, both in and out of the classroom. Here are steps you can take to help to develop more confidence:

- ✧ **Take a strengths inventory.** Make a list of what you're good at.
- ✧ **Set measurable, attainable goals.** Ask yourself what you want to accomplish in the next week, month, or year, and then break those goals up into smaller, short-term goals.
- ✧ **Take responsibility for your actions.** Make a consistent effort to learn from your experiences and choices—both the good and the bad.
- ✧ **Dare to take intellectual risks.** Question assumptions, and ask yourself if the things you believe to be true actually are.
- ✧ **Examine and acknowledge your feelings.** When something bothers you, try to identify why.
- ✧ **Take charge and be persistent.** Remember, luck is 99 percent perseverance.
- ✧ **Assert yourself.** When you want something, ask for it.
- ✧ **Remember, you're not alone.** Identify individuals who exhibit confidence, and make a strong effort to model the types of behavior that make the greatest impression on you.
- ✧ **Believe in yourself.**

## The Confidence Checklist

| | | |
|---|---|---|
| I believe I know what is best for me. | Yes | No |
| I feel I am a genuine person. | Yes | No |
| I am tolerant of others in my life. | Yes | No |
| I am consistent—I do as I say. | Yes | No |
| I avoid procrastinating. | Yes | No |
| I take an active role in class discussions. | Yes | No |
| I have an inner voice that guides my decisions. | Yes | No |

| | | |
|---|---|---|
| I maintain good eye contact and tone of voice when speaking. | Yes | No |
| I am able to handle constructive criticism. | Yes | No |
| I have difficulty trusting others. | Yes | No |
| I prefer being with people to being alone. | Yes | No |
| I would describe myself as an outgoing and assertive individual. | Yes | No |
| I am an optimistic person by nature. | Yes | No |

If you answered "No" to half or more of the statements, you might benefit from the strategies designed to boost your confidence. Read on!

##  2b Identify strengths and set goals

Why not start building your confidence by reminding yourself what you are good at? You can start with this simple, yet effective, activity:

**Make a list of what you believe are your strongest skills and qualities.** Take the time to think deeply and honestly about this exercise before you start. Another way to do this is to ask yourself: "When I feel like I am at my best, what am I doing?" Continue performing those activities to create an increased sense of confidence.

| **My strongest skills** | **My best qualities** |
|---|---|
| ____________________ | ____________________ |
| ____________________ | ____________________ |
| ____________________ | ____________________ |

**Long-term goals vs. short-term goals: How do they differ?** A critical part of developing, building, and maintaining your confidence is setting long- and short-term goals that you can reach and that are able to meet your expectations. Think of long-term goals as the final product and short-term goals as the steps along the way. For example, if you were to write a ten-chapter novel, you'd have ten short-term goals (write a chapter) and one long-term goal (write a novel).

## Goals worksheet

✧ Select one goal you would like to achieve in the next month. Be specific about what that goal is. ______________________________

✧ Now identify two or three effective actions you will take to obtain this goal. Once again, be specific and include a time frame for performing these actions.

______________________________

______________________________

______________________________

✧ Think of one possible barrier that might prevent you from reaching this goal.

______________________________

✧ Now consider one action you will take to overcome this barrier. Be sure to detail what this action will be. ______________________________

✧ Last, predict what you honestly believe will be your degree of success in achieving this goal. ______________________________

TIP *So how does setting goals help build confidence? Think about it this way: If you set up a series of short-term goals you know you can achieve, aren't you going to feel more confident each time you check off one of those goals? Even better, aren't you going to feel like a rock star by the time you achieve your ultimate long-term goal? There is nothing that builds more confidence than seeing hard work pay off.*

# 2c Learn from your experiences and choices

Wisdom can often be gained through both good and bad experiences and through the outcomes of the choices we make. If you can accept that you are ultimately the one responsible—not others—for your actions, this is the first important step to practicing this philosophy while in college.

One strategy for maintaining this belief is to not play the blame game; for example, if you received a low grade, be honest with yourself and ask what role you played in earning the grade. Admitting you are the one responsible for your actions and then responding (and learning) from that outcome will help strengthen your self-esteem and confidence.

**Taking risks** Has anyone ever told you, "Nothing ventured, nothing gained"? To take a risk can be an unsettling challenge—you can't be sure it will be worth it, you may question whether you have the ability and the desire to attempt something, and you might think about the consequences of that risk if you are unsuccessful.

Now, that's the negative approach. What if you turned this around and, instead, took a chance on something challenging? What if you decided that no matter what obstacles got in your way or what doubts crept into your mind, you would continue to pursue whatever you set out to accomplish? Imagine how you will feel when the results turn out to be positive ones.

Another way of thinking about risk is this: If you remain in your comfort zone you might never make any progress. While taking a risk can seem difficult at first, it almost always pays off in the end—especially in the classroom.

**Taking risks in the classroom** Your instructors have probably urged you to question rather than to simply accept everything you read or hear. If you follow this advice, you'll take risks in the classroom all the time—intellectual risks, otherwise known as critical thinking. You do this when you speak up in class, when you write an essay, and whenever you carefully rethink long-held beliefs.

**Speaking up in class** The reward for intellectual risk-taking is that you come away with a better understanding of yourself and the world around you. But what if you are terrified of speaking up in class and of saying something dumb? What if you simply don't know where to start? Here are two case studies to help you start thinking about how to better approach intellectual risks.

**Student A** read the class material twice and completed all the assignments. She came to class prepared to take notes and was ready and willing to listen to what the instructor had to say on the topic being presented. As an adult student, she was used to participating in meetings at work, and she didn't feel nervous about speaking up, so she didn't think that she needed to prepare any additional material.

**Student B** also completed the assigned homework and believed he knew the material but also knew he would be reluctant to share his thoughts or respond to questions posed to the class. As a strategy, he wrote down several questions and responses to what he assumed would be a part of the class discussion. When he attended class, he referred to his questions and answers when those areas of discussion came up.

What were some strategies that each student employed that would help them take intellectual risks? Who do you think came to class better prepared? For each case study, what would you recommend the student do differently next time?

**Preparing for class as a confidence boost** What do you do to prepare for class discussions? Try the following generic question starters to frame questions about the material covered. Then take a few minutes to jot down your answers.

> **What would happen if __________?**
>
> **What is the difference between __________ and __________?**
>
> **Why is __________ important?**
>
> **What is another way to look at __________?**
>
> **What did the author mean by __________?**

**Examining emotions** Daniel Goleman, author and creator of the theory of emotional intelligence (EQ), stresses the vital role EQ plays in building self-confidence. One of his key components is Emotional Self-Management, or the ability to make sensible decisions even when your emotions tell you to do otherwise. For example, if you received a failing grade on a quiz, your first impulse might be to get angry. Even worse, you might consider dropping the class. A better strategy would be to take the time to examine why you earned the grade that you did and to allow yourself the time needed to learn how to succeed in the course. Examining your feelings and how you react to certain situations can keep you from giving up too early on something that is challenging.

**Identifying confidence** Make a list of the qualities you see in people you think of as confident. Share the list with someone else in your class and discuss which of these qualities have to do with feelings and interactions with other people. How many of these qualities do you see in yourself?

**Being persistent** One of the simplest ways to gain confidence is to be persistent. *Persistence* simply means the ability to stick with something through completion, even if you don't always want to. If a task or challenge seems difficult at times and the outcome may be uncertain, persistence helps you keep at it. Let's look at an example:

Imagine that you are frustrated with the teaching style of one of your instructors. She presents the material in a way that doesn't work for you (but it seems to do so for your classmates). You can elect to drop the class early in the semester and perhaps have a different teacher next time, or you could take steps that will allow you to persist in the course, such as working with a tutor, forming a study group, or meeting with your professor for clarification. In the end, you will not have given up, and your outcome could likely be a favorable one.

Ultimately, it is *your* responsibility to take charge of your success and persist even if you have some setbacks at first. When you feel like you may be about to give up, remind yourself of your long-term goals and how persisting at the current task will help you attain those goals.

**Being assertive** One of the best ways to build confidence is to let people know what you want and don't want, how you feel, and when you need help. The more skilled you are at letting people know these things, the more assertive you'll become. The more you *successfully* assert yourself, the more confident you'll become. So how do you become more assertive? Let's start by assessing where you are right now.

## Assertiveness Check-Up

Answer the following questions as honestly as you can:

- Do you express your point of view even when it is not the same as others?
- Will you actually say "no" to a request made by friends or coworkers that you feel is unreasonable?
- How easily do you accept constructive criticism?
- Are you willing to ask for help?
- Do you make decisions or judgments with confidence?
- How open are you to another person's suggestions or advice?
- When you state your thoughts or feelings, do you do so in a direct and sincere manner?
- Are you likely to cooperate with others to achieve a worthwhile goal?

If you answered "yes" to less than half of the questions in the "Assertiveness Check-Up" box on the previous page, the strategies below can help you feel more confident when you are attempting to be assertive.

- Use suitable facial expressions.
- Always maintain good eye contact.
- Watch your tone of voice. Your voice should be firm, audible, and pleasant.
- Be aware of your body language—how you stand, sit, and gesture.
- Actively listen to others so that you can accurately confirm what they have said.
- Ask reasoned questions when something is unclear to you.
- Take a win-win approach to solving problems: How can what you're asking for benefit both you and the person you're asking?

## 2d Develop a network

When you create a supportive network of individuals, you are being interdependent, and this is a key to fostering self-confidence. By building mutually helpful relationships, you are more likely to achieve your goals and dreams. Here are some strategies for developing this interdependence:

- **Actively seek out your school's many resources.** This will mean connecting with an academic adviser, signing up for a tutor if you need one, or getting involved with several on- or off-campus activities.
- **Foster a valuable relationship with your instructors**; ask for their assistance, feedback, and constructive criticism.
- **Start a study group** by looking for several classmates who are prepared, regularly attend classes, and take an active part in class discussions. Don't overlook a quiet student who may have true insight into the course; that person can prove an asset. Approach those you've identified and suggest forming the group. If the answer is "yes," decide on your group's mutual goals and the rules your group will follow.

- **Don't be afraid to visit a counselor.** Coming to college can be a challenging and emotionally stressful experience; fortunately, your school offers counselors who can provide the understanding and skill to help you overcome your issues, so turning to one can be the right thing to do.

## Tips for confidence building

*Here are some proven strategies that will help you throughout your life. By following these steps, you will achieve* realistic and worthwhile *confidence:*

- As often as possible, focus on your strong points rather than areas of weakness. In other words, be aware of what is good about you and those things about you that you are proud of.
- Make a consistent effort to learn from your experiences—the good and bad.
- Find the courage to try something new and different, even when it appears difficult or risky.
- When something bothers or disappoints you, take the time to examine your thoughts. Choose to react calmly and rationally rather than on impulse and your emotions.
- Expect that while some of what you achieve in life may be due to pure luck, a good deal more will likely be the result of your personal persistence and effort.
- Strive to be assertive. This means express how you feel, what you think, the beliefs you hold, and do so directly and sincerely. You have a right to say "no" to requests that are not genuine or reasonable.
- Continue to learn and vary your skills and talents long after you leave college. Embrace the idea that there is no end to learning throughout your life.
- Most important of all, believe in yourself. Identify what distinguishes you from everyone else and what you have to offer. Once you know these qualities, you will begin to cultivate them by applying them in everyday life.

# CHAPTER 3
# Time management

You might be the kind of student who is content to spend hours making flashcards and outlining your notes in different colored ink. Or maybe you're good at channeling your adrenaline to start a lengthy source-based essay the night before it's due.

The problem is that both of these approaches carry risk. Procrastinate and you may pay for it when grades are posted. Do nothing but stare at your laptop in the library for weeks on end and you'll wind up dull, pasty, and miserable. If you're like most of us, you'll learn more, get better grades, and have more fun in college if you operate somewhere in the middle.

Most likely you've heard the Latin expression *carpe diem*, which translates to "seize the day" (as in, make time work for you). Mastering the art of time management is one key to your future success and happiness, but learning to make time work for you can be a challenge.

## 3a The case for time management

*Why bother?* We know. Some students don't want to "waste" time on planning and managing their schedules. Instead, they prefer to tackle tasks and responsibilities as they come up. Unfortunately, the demands of college (not to mention most careers) require serious, intentional strategies. Since not many of us can afford to hire a personal assistant, it's worthwhile to be a bit more responsible about managing time. Bad habits from the past may not carry you through.

*To psych yourself up, think of time management as part of your life skill set.* If you're trying to remember all the things you need to get done, it's hard to focus on actually doing the work. Organizing your time well accomplishes three things. First, it optimizes your chances of getting good results by ensuring that you're not rushing tasks or missing deadlines. Second, it enhances your life by saving you from stress and regret. And finally, it reflects what you value. It's all about doing your best.

*Remember that people who learn good time management techniques in college generally soar in their careers.* If you're more efficient at your job, you'll be able to accomplish more. That will lend you a competitive advantage over your coworkers. Your bosses will learn to depend on you, and they may reward you with interesting projects, promotions, and educational and training opportunities. You'll feel empowered and positive—and may even have more time for a social life, which has been shown to lower stress and advance careers.

## 3b Taking charge of your time

Freedom can be a dangerous thing. One of the biggest differences between high school and college is that you find yourself, as a college student, with far more independence—and greater responsibility—than you've ever known. If you are continuing your education after a break, you may be contending with family or work obligations, too. But it would be a mistake to assume that Oprah, rocket scientists, and other type-A folks have some kind of monopoly on organization and focus. You, the ordinary student, can also embrace your inner executive assistant—the one who keeps you on time, on task, and ready for what comes next. So how do you begin?

**Set some goals.** Goals help you figure out where to devote the majority of your time. To achieve your goals, you need to do more than just think about them. You need to act. This requires setting both short- and long-term goals. When you are determining your long-term goals, it is important to be honest and realistic with yourself. Goals should be challenging, but they should also be attainable. Be sure they align with your abilities, values, and interests. Do you want to go on to further schooling? Have you decided what career you want to pursue? Mulling over these questions can help you start thinking about where you want to be in the next five to ten years. Dreaming up long-term goals can be exciting and fun; however, reaching your goals requires undertaking a number of steps in the short term.

*Try to be very specific* when determining your short-term goals. For example, if you're committed to becoming an expert in a certain field, you'll want to commit yourself to every class and internship that can help you on your way. A specific goal would be to review your school's course catalog, identify the courses you want to take, and determine when you must take them. An even more specific goal would be to research interesting internship opportunities in your field of study. The good news about goals is that all the small steps add up.

**Identify five short-term goals—goals you believe you can accomplish in the next six to twelve months.**

1. ______________________________

2. ______________________________

3. ______________________________

4. ______________________________

5. ______________________________

**Identify one long-term goal—one that you'd like to accomplish in the next several years.**

______________________________

______________________________

**Now identify three steps that will move you toward your long-term goal.**

1. ______________________________

2. ______________________________

3. ______________________________

**Know your priorities.** To achieve your goals, set your life priorities so that you're steadily working toward them.

- **Start out with a winner's mentality.** Make sure your studies are your priority. Having worked so hard to get to college, you cannot allow Netflix binge watching and other activities derail your schoolwork. Review your current commitments and prepare to sacrifice a few—for now. Whatever you do, talk to your family, your boss, and your friends about your college workload and goals so that everyone's on the same page. When you have a looming deadline, be firm. Emphasize that no amount of badgering will succeed in getting you to go to the *Stranger Things* theme party during finals week.
- **Next, start preparing for your future.** Visit your campus career center and schedule an assessment test to hone in on your talents and interests. Or, if you know what career you want to pursue, talk with a professional in that field, your guidance counselor, a professor, or an upper-class student in your chosen major to find out what steps you need to take to get the results you want, starting now. What skills and experiences should be on your résumé when you graduate that will make you stand out from the pack? Make a plan, prioritize your goals, and then make a time management schedule.
- **Balance is key.** Being realistic about your future and goals may mean making big sacrifices. Be realistic about the present, too. Always include time in your schedule for people who are important to you and time on your own to recharge.

> TIP
>
> **Share your Google or Outlook calendar.** *Keeping an electronic copy of your calendar allows you to share it with others at a click of a button. Letting your family, friends, and employer know what is on your plate at any given moment can prevent misunderstandings from arising because of your school commitments and create a more supportive home and work environment.*

**Embrace the 2-for-1 rule.** For every hour you spend in class at college, you should plan to study two hours outside of class. That's the standard, so keep it in mind when you're planning your schedule. The bottom line is that you carry more responsibility for your education in college than you did in high school.

**Own your class schedule.** Your schedule will affect almost every aspect of your college life. Before you register, think about how to make your schedule work for you.

- ✧ **Start with your biorhythms.** Do you study more effectively in the day or the evening? Or is it a combination of both? Ideally, you should devote your peak hours—when you're most alert and engaged—to schoolwork. Schedule other activities, like doing laundry, emailing, exercising, and socializing, for times when it's harder to concentrate. Start by filling out the chart on page 22.

- ✧ **If you live on campus**, you might want to create a schedule that situates you near a dining hall at mealtimes or lets you spend breaks between classes at the library. Feel free to slot breaks for relaxation and catching up with friends. Embrace the midday nap, but make it brief. Research shows that if the nap is longer than thirty minutes, you risk feeling lethargic afterward or, even worse, oversleeping and missing a class. If you attend a large college or university, be sure to allow adequate time to get from one class to another.

- ✧ **Try to alternate classes with free periods.** Also, seek out instructors who'll let you attend lectures at alternative times if you're absent. If they offer flexibility in due dates for assignments, all the better. If you're a commuter student, you might be tempted to schedule your classes in blocks without breaks. But before you do this, consider the following:
  - The fatigue factor
  - No last-minute study periods before tests
  - The possibility of having several exams on the same day
  - In case of illness, falling behind in all classes

With your own **biorhythms and preferences** in mind, fill out the chart on the following page. Use check marks to match up typical activities with *your* best time of day to do these activities.

| | *Early morning 3–8 a.m.* | *Morning 8 a.m.–12 p.m.* | *Midday 12–5 p.m.* | *Evening 5–11 p.m.* | *Late night 11 p.m.–3 a.m.* |
|---|---|---|---|---|---|
| ***Exercise*** | | | | | |
| ***Classes*** | | | | | |
| ***Homework*** | | | | | |
| ***Appointments*** | | | | | |
| ***Errands*** | | | | | |
| ***Job*** | | | | | |
| ***Socializing*** | | | | | |
| ***Laundry, paying bills, etc.*** | | | | | |
| ***Sleep*** | | | | | |

## Control factor: Know what you **can** and **can't** control

*When it comes to planning your time, it helps to know the difference between what you can control and what you can't control.*

### What you **can** control

- **Making good choices.** How often do you say "I don't have time"? Probably a lot. But truth be told, you have a choice when it comes to most of the major commitments in your life. You also control many of the small decisions that keep you focused on your goals: when you wake up, how much sleep you get, what you eat, how much time you spend studying, and whether you get exercise. Be a person with a plan. If you want something, make time for it.
- **Doing your part to succeed.** Go to all your classes; arrive on time; buy all the required textbooks; keep track of your activities; complete every reading and writing assignment on time; take notes in class; and, whenever possible, participate and ask questions.
- **Managing your stress levels.** Organization is the key to tranquility and positive thinking. Manage your time well, and you won't be tormented with thoughts of all the things that need doing. Want to avoid unnecessary stress? Plan ahead.

### What you **can't** control

- **Knowing how much you'll need to study right away.** Depending on the kind of high school you went to (and the types of courses you took there) and how long it has been since you've had to study, you might be more or less prepared than your college classmates. If your studying or writing skills lag behind, expect to put in a little extra time until you're up to speed.
- **Running into scheduling conflicts.** If you find it hard to get the classes you need, you can seek help from a dean, an academic adviser, or someone in the college counseling center.
- **Needing a job to help pay your way.** Just follow the experts' rule of thumb: If you're taking a full course load, do your best to avoid working more than fifteen hours a week. Any more than that and your academic work could suffer.

## 3c Four time-wasting habits to avoid

**1. Procrastinating** Maybe you're a perfectionist—in which case, avoiding a task might be easier than having to live up to your own very high expectations (or those of your parents or instructors). Maybe you object to the sheer dullness of an assignment, or you think you can learn the material just as well without doing the work. Maybe you even fear success and know just how to subvert it.

None of these qualify as valid reasons to put off your work. They're just excuses that will get you in trouble. Fortunately, doing tasks you don't like is excellent practice for real life.

*Tips to Stop Procrastination*

- **Break big jobs down into smaller chunks.** Spend only a few minutes planning your strategy and then act on it.
- **Reward yourself** for finishing a task. For example, you might watch your favorite TV show or play a game with your kids or friends.
- **Find a quiet, comfortable place to work** that doesn't allow for distractions and interruptions. Don't listen to music or keep the TV on. If you study in your room, shut the door.
- **Treat your study time as a serious commitment.** That means no phone calls, email, text messages, or social media updates. You can rejoin society later.
- **Consider the consequences if you don't get down to work.** You don't want to let bad habits hamper your ability to achieve good results *and* have a life.

**2. Overextending yourself** Although what constitutes a realistic workload varies significantly from one person to another, feeling overextended is a huge source of stress for college students. Being involved in campus life is fun and important, but it's crucial not to let your academic work take a backseat.

- **Learn to say no—even if it means letting other people down.** Don't be tempted to compromise your priorities.

- **But don't give up all nonacademic pursuits.** Students who work or participate in extracurricular activities often achieve higher grades than their less active counterparts partly because of the important role that time management plays in their lives.

- **If you're truly overloaded with commitments and can't see a way out,** you may need to drop a course before the drop deadline. It may seem drastic, but a low grade on your permanent record is even worse. Become familiar with your school's add/drop policy to avoid penalties. If you receive financial aid, keep in mind that in most cases you must be registered for a minimum number of credit hours to be considered a full-time student and maintain your current level of aid.

**3. Losing your focus** Some first-year college students lose sight of their goals. They spend their first term blowing off classes and assignments, then either get placed on probation or have to spend years clawing their way back to a decent GPA. So plan your strategy and keep yourself focused and motivated for the long haul.

**4. Running late** Punctuality is a virtue. Rolling in late to class or review sessions shows a lack of respect for both your instructors and your classmates. Arrive early to class and avoid using your phone, texting, doing homework for another class, falling asleep, talking, whispering, or running out to feed a parking meter. Part of managing your time is freeing yourself to focus on the present and on other people who inhabit the present with you. Note: Respecting others is a habit that can work wonders in your career and personal life.

## 3d Two tools to keep you on track

Once you enter college or the working world, adopt a habit of writing down everything you need to do, prioritizing your tasks, and leaving yourself frequent reminders. The good news is that a little up-front planning will make your life infinitely easier and more relaxing. For one thing, you'll be less likely to make mistakes. On top of that, you'll free your brain from having to remember all the things you need to get done so that you can focus on actually doing the work. Two key items will help you plan to succeed.

**A planner or calendar** Find out if your campus bookstore sells a planner with important school-specific dates and deadlines already marked. Or, if you prefer to use an online calendar or the one that comes on your smartphone, that's fine too. As you schedule your time, follow a few basic guidelines:

*Pick the timeframe that works best for you.* If you want a "big picture" sense of how your schedule plays out, try setting up a calendar for the whole term or for the month. For a more detailed breakdown of what you need to accomplish in the near future, a calendar for the week or even the day may be a better fit. If you're keeping your calendar on a smartphone, you can toggle among different views—day, week, and month.

*Enter all of your commitments.* Once you've selected your preferred time frame, record your commitments and other important deadlines. These might include your classes, assignment due dates, work hours, family commitments, and so on. Be specific. For instance, "Read Chapter 8 in history" is preferable to "Study history," which is better than simply "Study." Include meeting times and locations, social events, and study time for each class. Take advantage of your smartphone by setting reminders and alerts to keep you on top of all your activities and obligations.

*Break large assignments like research projects into smaller bits,* such as choosing a topic, doing research, creating an outline, learning necessary computer skills, writing a first draft, and so on. Estimate how much time each assignment will take you. Give yourself deadlines, then start as far ahead of that deadline as you can. A good time manager often finishes projects before the actual due dates to allow for emergencies.

*Watch out for your toughest weeks during the term.* If you find that paper deadlines and test dates fall during the same week or even the same day, you can minimize some of the stress by finding time to finish other assignments early to free up time for study and writing. If there's a major conflict, talk it over with your professor. Professors will be more likely to help you if you talk with them early instead of at the last minute.

*Update your planner/calendar frequently.* Enter all due dates as soon as you know them. Be obsessive about this.

*Check your planner/calendar every day* (at the same time of day if that helps you remember). You'll want to review the current week and the next week, too.

*When in doubt, turn to a type-A classmate for advice.* A hyper-organized friend can be your biggest ally when it comes to making a game plan.

**A to-do list** The easiest way to remember all the things you need to do is to jot them down on a running to-do list—updating as needed. You can do this on paper or use an online calendar or smartphone to record the day's obligations.

1. **Prioritize.** Rank items on your list in order of importance. Alternatively, circle or highlight urgent tasks.
2. **Every time you complete a task, cross it off the list.**
3. **Move undone items to the top of your next list.**
4. **Start a new to-do list every day or once a week.** It shouldn't be just about academics. Slot in errands you need to run, appointments you need to schedule, emails you need to send, and anything else you need to do that day or week.

## Resources

| | |
|---|---|
| Control of the Study Environment | **www.ucc.vt.edu/academic_support/study_skills_information/control_of_study_environment.html** |
| Mind Tools for Getting the Most Out of Your Time | **www.mindtools.com/page5.html** |
| Mobile Student Planner | **www.istudentpro.com** |
| Printable Checklists | **www.allfreeprintables.com/checklists/to-do-lists.shtml** |
| Student Organizer | **www.primasoft.com/so.htm** |

# CHAPTER 4

# College ethics and personal responsibility

As a college student, it's important for you to understand what kinds of behaviors are considered academic dishonesty or, more to the point, cheating. Unfortunately, technology has made it easier than ever for students to cheat. However, it's also much easier for colleges to catch students who cheat. College administrators are cracking down on cheating by making the penalties increasingly harsh.

To complicate matters, some students cheat without even knowing that they're cheating. Often it happens when a student doesn't know or doesn't understand the rules about using other people's work. At some schools, teachers and administrators are more lenient with these students, but it's better not to count on leniency. It's better to know the rules, the consequences, and some strategies for avoiding cheating.

##  4a What is cheating?

Cheating comes in two forms: faking your own work and helping other students fake theirs.

### Some of the most obvious forms of cheating

- Buying an essay from someone else
- Texting answers during an exam

- Sharing the details of a test with students who haven't taken it yet
- Copying someone else's homework
- Peeking at someone else's test paper
- Letting other people cheat from your work
- Stealing a test
- Writing answers to the test in tiny letters on your gum wrappers or on the inside of your bottled water label (Note: Professors know these tricks.)

**Plagiarism: The most common form of cheating** The trouble with plagiarism is that many students don't completely understand what it is. Plagiarism, according to the *Oxford English Dictionary*, is "taking someone else's work, idea, etc., and passing it off as one's own."

Does anyone *really* think it's OK to copy whole sentences from the Internet and paste them into their essays? Some people don't think twice about downloading copyrighted music, so it could be that the concepts of *ownership* and *borrowing* aren't as clear as they used to be. Perhaps personal responsibility is muddy when it comes to intellectual property. What's your stance? Have you ever lifted a passage from a website, maybe even changing words to make it sound more like you? Do you believe that once something is on the web, it's in the public domain? Copying or paraphrasing anything from the Internet, or from any other source, and using it without citing the source is plagiarism.

*Be responsible:* Plagiarizing with intent is one thing. Many college students are accused of plagiarism simply because they are being irresponsible and forget to define which parts of an essay are their own and which parts belong to another author. It's in your best interest to seek out your school's plagiarism policy and definitions.

**I have viewed and understand my school's plagiarism policy and the consequences of submitting plagiarized work as my own.**

**Signed:** ______________________________ **Date:** ____________

## 4b The case for integrity

Cheating is wrong, and it doesn't represent the hard work needed for success in school and beyond. Getting caught could set off a firestorm and seriously affect your future. What's worse, cheating is bad for your self-image and can trigger both guilt and anxiety.

Because attending college is ultimately about learning new things, challenging yourself, and building your integrity, you defeat the whole point if you try to get through dishonestly. Here's the sobering reality: Cheating has a nasty way of seeping into other parts of your life, like your career, your finances, and your personal relationships, where it can cause long-term damage. But integrity can seep as well. If you conduct your academic life with honesty and live as a college student with principles, chances are you'll be seen as honest and principled in your personal and professional lives as well.

## 4c Tools teachers use when they suspect cheating

College professors can easily investigate their suspicions, and nowadays they have better resources to back them up. Programs like Turnitin.com let instructors scan essays and crosscheck them against books, newspapers, journals, and student papers, as well as against material that's publicly accessible on the web. Even without such a program, a teacher can put a suspicious passage into a Google search and turn up possible plagiarism. Just a brief, single-sentence snippet could give you away. In short, don't risk getting caught. If you're overwhelmed, meet with your teacher and discuss it. Or take a trip to the writing center and work through citing sources with one of the tutors. Know some alternatives so that the possibility of getting caught isn't causing you anxiety.

## 4d How to be a more responsible student: Ten tips

1. **Avoid friends who pressure you to bend the rules.** Writing a paper is really hard. Doing advanced math and science homework is really hard. Studying for exams is lonely, boring, and *really* hard. But trying to beat the system doesn't pay. Remind

yourself of the consequences of cheating. Explain to your friends that you are on a valiant quest for honest effort.

2. **Join a study group.** If you're struggling to get through a course, get together with other students to compare notes and help each other grasp tricky concepts. A study group gives you a support system and a more positive belief in yourself. It teaches you persistence and discipline because the group structure involves meeting promptly at set times for reviews. A study group can also make learning easier and more fun.
3. **Don't procrastinate.** If you want to write a thorough and honest essay, you need to start early. College papers aren't like movie reviews. You're often required to locate, read, and evaluate sources. Next, you have to integrate evidence from sources into an outline, a first draft, and ultimately an original work with a central claim. All of that takes time. If you leave things until it is too late, you'll be more tempted to cheat.
4. **Don't muddle your notes.** It's vital that you keep your own writing separate from the material you've gathered from other sources. Why? Because it's surprisingly easy to mistake someone else's words for your own, especially after you get two hours into writing and your brain turns numb. So document everything.
5. **Be a stickler about internal citation.** It happens all the time. At the end of an essay, a student provides a full works cited list, including all the works quoted, summarized, or paraphrased. But in the paper itself, there are no citations to be found. Using phrases that signal the switch from your idea to a source's idea—along with the page number of the source (if one is available)—can make a big difference. In this example from the body of a student paper, the writer uses internal citation along with a signal phrase.

    **Surprisingly, students in reduced meal programs don't always participate. According to a recent report from the Food Research and Action Center, "stigma and the allure of competitive foods" decrease student participation in the program (10).**

6. **Familiarize yourself with the proper formatting for a research paper.** MLA style is widely used in classes such as English and composition; if your instructors require a different style, they will let you know. Your handbook is an excellent tool for

learning the basic guidelines and rules for citations. You might also want to speak to a reference librarian, an expert in gathering research and someone who can be one of your biggest allies in college. Alternatively, pay a visit to the writing center on campus or talk to your instructor for advice.

7. **Be sure to list all of the sources you quoted, summarized, or paraphrased in your works cited list.** Sources should be listed alphabetically in proper MLA format. If you're not sure how to list a citation or if you're not sure that your source information is valid, don't just leave it out and keep your fingers crossed.
8. **Master the art of paraphrasing.** Paraphrasing is restating someone else's ideas or observations in your own words. Paraphrasing involves understanding the original passage and presenting it in your own way. You don't have to put the text in quotation marks, but a citation acknowledging the original source is still required.
9. **If you need help, seek it early.** This sounds obvious, but it's important to go to the writing center or the librarian well before your paper is actually due. Review and revision take time—and chances are your paper will benefit from outside help.
10. **If you hand something in and then realize that you used material without giving credit to the source, alert your instructor immediately.** We repeat: Don't just hope it will slip through. Better to risk half a grade point on one essay than a larger consequence such as failing the course.

## 4e How to paraphrase (to avoid plagiarism)

Paraphrasing doesn't mean copying a quotation and switching the words around. It doesn't mean changing two or three words in a sequence, either. It means rephrasing and restructuring someone else's idea altogether while retaining its meaning. Paraphrasing requires you, as a writer, to understand the author's meaning and then present it in your own words and in your own sentence structure. Consider these examples:

QUOTATION "The jobs growth forecast for the auto industry appears dim."

PARAPHRASE We will see a decrease in the number of available jobs at the biggest carmakers.

QUOTATION "Google has been working to build cars that drive themselves."

PARAPHRASE One of Google's latest projects is a robotic car that takes humans out of the driver's seat.

If you're having trouble paraphrasing something, try this strategy: Put away your source material, call up a friend or your mom, and explain the point you're trying to summarize. Chances are you'll come away with something that's clear and concise, that's in your own words, and that reflects your own presentation of the ideas.

Keep in mind that when you paraphrase someone else's words, you still have to cite the source.

TIP *When copying research material into your notes, write the name of the source and the page number directly after it. Likewise, when you copy something from the Internet, add a URL. Use quotation marks around all cited material. Also try highlighting your research in a bright color to set it apart from your notes. All of this will make writing your draft easier.*

**PRACTICE ✦** Paraphrase this passage from earlier in this chapter.

> **If you're struggling to get through a course, get together with other students to compare notes and help each other grasp tricky concepts. A study group gives you a support system and a more positive belief in yourself. It teaches you persistence and discipline because the group structure involves meeting promptly at set times for reviews. A study group can also make learning easier and more fun.**

According to advice by Bedford/St. Martin's, ______________________________

______________________________________________________________

______________________________________________________________

______________________________________________________________

______________________________________________________________

____________________________________________________________(34).

## 5c Classroom rules

Your instructors care about your future and will be willing to meet with you before or after class. However, they aren't accountable for your success or failure. Following a few rules will show that you are prepared to command your own success.

1. **Show up.** Attendance is important. Missing one day in college is like missing a week of high school because everything is so much more concentrated.
2. **Show up on time.** Plan your commute and arrange your courses so that you can get to class right on schedule. Ideally, you want to arrive a few minutes early so that you can calmly find a seat and take out your book, laptop, and other supplies.
3. **Come prepared.** If you've been assigned reading or homework, have it done in advance.
4. **Pay close attention to the syllabus.** The syllabus spells out exactly what's required of you if you're going to succeed in the class. The syllabus often lists readings, assignments, policies, and the instructor's contact information.
5. **Expect to work.** You're not entitled to a passing grade merely because you show up to class or because you've paid for the credits. To succeed, you need to participate in discussions, take notes, study, do well on tests, and complete all of your assignments. If you're sinking, talk to your professor during office hours. There's an incredible amount of help on college campuses: writing centers, math tutors, language labs for nonnative English speakers, and academic advisers.
6. **Don't surf the web.** Taking notes on your laptop is fine. Checking your email or Twitter feed is not. These activities distract other students, and professors view such activity as rude.
7. **Don't try to monopolize the conversation.** You're in class to learn something, right? So find a balance between participation in the discussion and active listening. While you're at it, be a great listener in study groups, too.

## 5d Collaborating with others: The group project

Today, most college classes involve doing hands-on projects in small groups. The shift to a more learner-centered classroom environment is a response to the idea that classroom demands should, in part, prepare you for workplace demands. Team settings, common in the workplace, involve a new kind of etiquette.

- **Treat the students in your group as teammates.** It's vital that you pull your weight, come to meetings on time, listen to what others have to say, and plan together. A group project should be collaborative, not competitive. You're all working toward the same goal, and part of your grade may be based on your teamwork skills.
- **Give constructive criticism.** If you're required to offer a peer review of an essay, stay neutral and focused, and don't get personal. It's helpful to use "I" statements. For example, "I'm confused" is better than "This paper is confusing." Also, it helps to keep to specifics: What did you like best about the essay and why? Where would you like to know more information?
- **Prepare to learn from each other.** The fact that the people in your group have different backgrounds and talents — but are interested in the same subject — already makes for a creative group dynamic. Chances are, testing ideas out with classmates will make you smarter and broaden your world view.

## 5e Communicating with your professor

Most instructors are passionate about their subject matter and appreciate and enjoy students. Make a habit of talking with them occasionally outside of class.

- **Discover office hours.** Almost all instructors post days and times when they're available to students. If those hours don't work for you, you can always ask to schedule an appointment. Attending office hours is one of the best learning tools you have in college. Visit early in the semester for quick check-ins — don't wait until just before an exam or the due date for an essay.
- **Embrace your college email account.** Check your college email account often for updates, even if you do not use it regularly in your life outside of school. Your instructors may use the tool to send information about assignments, activities, and canceled classes. Used properly, it can be a great way to communicate with your professor, too.

- **Don't expect your instructor to call you back after work.** Many college faculty members are careful not to call students back from home because they don't want their private numbers made public and because they don't want to seem unprofessional. If you leave a message for your professor, either by phone or email, it could be a full twenty-four hours before they contact you.
- **If you have a personal crisis, head to the office** for a face-to-face meeting. If you find yourself in an exceptional situation that is affecting your class work, talk to your instructor in private, not in the classroom with nineteen other people listening. Most teachers will work with you.

## Serious mistakes

- **Disappearing.** It happens more often than you'd think: Students attend class for a couple of weeks and then vanish into thin air. Keep in mind that the college disappearing act can affect your financial aid.
- **Not staying in touch with your professors.** If you must be away or you have a conflict with an exam, make arrangements with your instructor ahead of time. It's important to do this well in advance.
- **Blatant rudeness.** Some behavior—chronic lateness, obvious texting, being abusive to other students in a debate—is virtually apology-resistant.

## The right way to ask for a reference

- **Give your professor two to four weeks' lead time.** It takes thought and research to write a good reference, and your instructor might have to unearth your file from a few semesters back. Keep in mind that college faculty members are busy people.
- **Provide instructions for online submission—or a stamped envelope.** Your instructor shouldn't have to scramble. The easier you make it for your instructor to submit the reference, the more time they have to focus on praise for your accomplishments and efforts.
- **Be thorough about what the application is for**, what the organization wants to know about you, and where the reference needs to be sent.

## Have a complaint?

- **Talk to your instructor privately**, during office hours.
- **Speak in *I* messages, not *you* messages.** *You* messages ("You never explained this stuff") sound inherently hostile and tend to put people on the offensive. *I* messages, on the other hand, simply state a problem ("I feel frustrated because we never touched on logical fallacies in class, yet there was a question about it on the test").
- **Resist the urge to vent about your professor on the Internet.** Online discussion groups and social websites are not the place to whine about your school, your instructor, or your fellow students. That's what calling home is for. Everything posted to the web is public.

## How to write to your professor

*These three words can be a simple guideline: Use formal English. Using shorthand or text slang can affect your professor's attitude toward you—and not in a good way. Consider a few examples of actual student emails:*

Acceptable:

Dear Professor Fuller,

This is David K. I am in your TR 11:30–12:45 Eng-091 Class. I was unable to attend class this morning due to a bad reaction I had to some food I ate last night. I was in the ER this morning. I was wondering if it is at all possible to know what the lesson was on today and I will work on it during the weekend. I know I will not get credit for it but I would like to work on it anyway.

Thank you,

David

Unacceptable:

hi is april are u gonna send us the homework so i can print it out and show u it

Unacceptable: Hello Fuller,

I'm sorry to not come today I was just wondering if I can take the gammar test tomorrow in your moring class please. My mom Got Rush to the hospital. I promise I will not miss no more classes. I know this is my third time but im trying to do good. So please can you get back to me asap. Nicki

---

**Being gracious to your academic adviser: A how-to** When you visit your academic adviser, you can't present yourself like a blank slate and expect your adviser to sketch out your future. The smart, polite thing to do is to prepare before the meeting. Tell your adviser what classes you're interested in and which majors you're considering. Know your work schedule so that you can pick classes that don't conflict with your job. If you're saying to yourself, "I have no idea which direction to go," spend some time in the career center. Then meet with your academic adviser, ask thoughtful questions, and listen.

**PRACTICE** ✦ Rewrite the following email to a professor using a professional tone, proper formatting, and Standard English. Feel free to invent a name for the professor and any other details you think the message may need.

> **Hey i am applying for the dean's team so I can b a mentor for incoming students in the Bus. School. i need a recomendtion from a teacher and you now me well i have a good grade in yr class would you write it thanks!**

PART 2
*Succeeding in Your Writing Course*

## CHAPTER 6

# Developing active reading strategies

College assignments require you to read deeply and thoroughly, analyzing what you read for various purposes. Your composition instructor may ask you to analyze a writer's claims and support for an argument, evaluating the writer's choices and their effectiveness in convincing readers. A history instructor may assign a research topic, asking you to analyze the major causes of the Civil War and its effects on society today. In your economics class, you may be asked to write a paper in which you compare the theories of two prominent economists.

## 6a On-ramps for reading assignments

The better you understand a reading, the better prepared you will be to handle academic reading and writing assignments. It may be tempting to skip the reading and go straight to writing or to read just the first page or two of an article, but without a clear understanding of the assigned reading or any additional sources you gather at the library or online, you will have difficulty completing your academic assignments successfully.

The following strategies will help you dig in to what you read. The particular strategy steps you use will depend on your reading task. With practice, you will gain confidence and efficiency in choosing and using effective, active reading strategies. Think of deep strategic reading as looking for on-ramps to a reading that will help you understand it. Not all readings will require the same on-ramps, so you will have to be flexible. You may need to approach one reading differently than you approach another. Your goal, of course, is to understand a reading from start to finish.

This chapter covers five on-ramps for active, strategic reading:

- Pay attention to titles.
- Read for patterns.
- Understand vocabulary.
- Identify main ideas.
- Outline what you read.

## 6b Pay attention to titles

Titles give readers their first clues to the writer's purpose, audience, and thesis. Consider the following titles carefully. With a partner, describe what you expect to read about. (See additional activities on page 147.)

a. "Growing Global Water Scarcity Creates a New Breed of Criminal: Will You Become One?"

_______________

_______________

b. "Parenting Styles Linked to Teen Distracted Driving"

_______________

_______________

c. "How Suburban Landscaping Is Increasing Disease-Carrying Populations of Mosquitoes and Why Solutions Are Costly to Pursue"

TIP *Learn as much as you can about the publication (the website, journal, magazine, or newspaper) in which a reading appears, the publication date, and the author. Information about the publication and the author provides added clues to the writer's purpose and intended audience. You should reflect on the publication date, considering how the issue may have changed since the piece was written.*

**WRITING ACTIVITY ✦ Using a title as an on-ramp**

Find an article on a local or national news website (NPR, CNN, *The Washington Post*). Copy the name of the article here, but don't read the article.

With just the title and the publication in mind, describe what you expect to read about.

## 6c Read for patterns

Writers organize their ideas into logical patterns to communicate the ideas clearly to readers. Narration is one logical pattern. A narrative is often organized chronologically (that is, in order by time): beginning, middle, and end. Reading for patterns will help you follow the logic of what you read.

Consider the following patterns and transition words/phrases that writers, you included, rely on to organize ideas. Think of finding patterns in a writer's work as reverse analysis. Everything you read was written by someone who had to decide how to organize ideas in a way that readers would understand.

| Pattern | *How the pattern unlocks the writer's purpose* | *Key questions to consider when reading a work with this pattern* | *Typical transition words* |
|---|---|---|---|
| ***Narration*** | Lets a writer tell a story or show how events unfold in time order | What are the events of the story?<br>Why is this story being told? | first, second, as, during, after, next, meanwhile, finally, when, while |
| ***Description*** | Provides details that bring a person, place, or thing to life | What details and language are being used and why?<br>What is the emotional or sensory impact of this description? | above, below, beyond, near, nearby, in, inside, similarly, likewise |
| ***Illustration*** | Supports an idea, argument, or proposal with examples | How does this illustration make things clear to me? | for example, for instance, in particular, to illustrate, in other words, in fact, specifically |
| ***Classification*** | Sorts people, things, or ideas into categories | What are the categories?<br>Is this the way I would group these subjects? | first, second, finally, similarly, likewise, however, on one hand, on the other hand, but, although |
| ***Definition*** | Puts a thing or idea in a general class and adds details to distinguish it from others in its class | What is the general class?<br>Do the details give me a better sense of what this thing or idea is? | for example, and, but, however |
| ***Process*** | Describes a process or shows readers, step by step, how to do something | What are the steps?<br>Are the steps clear and logical? | first, next, then, after, as, while, when, meanwhile, finally |

| Pattern | How the pattern unlocks the writer's purpose | Key questions to consider when reading a work with this pattern | Typical transition words |
|---|---|---|---|
| **Compare/ Contrast** | Lets a writer show how two people, places, things, or ideas are similar to and/or different from each other | What similarities/ differences are being listed?<br>What seems important about these similarities/ differences? | also, and, similarly, likewise, but, yet, however, on the other hand, in contrast, even though |
| **Cause/Effect** | Shows the factors that led to or might lead to an outcome or shows the possible results of a certain cause | What reasons or factors are given?<br>What positive or negative outcomes are listed? | therefore, if, so, for, thus, because, since |

TIP *Writers seldom use only one pattern to organize their ideas for readers. Anticipate that more than one pattern is being employed. When you are writing, challenge yourself to use more than one pattern in brainstorming and organizing your ideas as well.*

**WRITING ACTIVITY ✦ Using patterns as an on-ramp**

Label patterns in the margin of your reading and use them to explain the writer's point. See chapter 15 for readings you can practice with.

## 6d Understand vocabulary

Throughout your reading process, make the time to look up words you don't know. To save time and effort, have an online dictionary open when you read so that you can look up words quickly. If more than one definition is offered, consider which definition best fits the sentence. Write that definition in the margin or in the space above the word. Strong readers generally take the time to look up words they do not know, and over time they increase their vocabulary.

A popular timesaver is to search for context clues—clues to a word's definition, found in the sentence where the word occurs or in the sentences around it. Use context clues to determine the definition of the word *reminisce* in the following passage from "My Pilgrimage" by student Jasen Berverly:

> **Upon reaching Downtown Crossing at 7:45, I exit the train and begin to watch as people dart down the long corridor in hopes of catching the train. This becomes the highlight of the morning as I watch the doors slam in people's faces. There's no explaining the humor of watching people who have tried so hard, panting angrily as the train leaves without them.**
>
> **Standing on the platform, I recognize a few familiar faces. They belong to students of Charlestown High School. I laugh, knowing that school for them began at 7:20. Then I begin to reminisce about my own CHS experiences. I think about all my suspension hearings, the work I refused to do, and how easy it was to get by doing the bare minimum. Only the cold draft of the approaching train brings me back to reality.**

The following sentence provides the clue that *to reminisce* means to think about one's past: "I think about all my suspension hearings, the work I refused to do, and how easy it was to get by doing the bare minimum."

#### WRITING ACTIVITY ✦ Using vocabulary as an on-ramp

Fill the spaces between lines of text with definitions of words you don't know. Underline or circle clues to difficult or technical terms. See chapter 15 for readings you can practice with.

##  6e Identify main ideas

Consider how paragraphs begin and end. Note that the first or last sentence in a paragraph often presents the overall idea of the paragraph. Understanding the main idea in each paragraph will give you clues about the major ideas in a complete reading. Consider the following paragraph from a chapter in a history textbook:

> **While women's influence was praised in the post–Revolutionary era, state laws rarely expanded women's rights. All states limited women's economic autonomy, although a few allowed married women to enter into business. Divorce was also legalized in many states but was still available only to the wealthy and well connected. Meanwhile women were excluded from juries, legal training, and, with rare exceptions, voting rights.**
>
> *Source*: Hewitt, Nancy A., and Steven F. Lawson. *Exploring American Histories*, 2nd ed., Bedford/St. Martin's, p. 160.

This paragraph gives some sense of what women's lives were like in the early days of our nation. You may suspect that the larger reading addresses the growing influence of women in America, even with the limitations mentioned in this paragraph.

### WRITING ACTIVITY ✦ Using main ideas as an on-ramp

Challenge yourself to mark or write down the main idea of each paragraph. You may decide that two or more paragraphs work as a unit to convey one main point. See chapter 15 for readings you can practice with.

## 6f Outline what you read

Another active reading strategy is to create an outline in the margins that labels the content of the reading from start to finish (main idea, important evidence, "reason #2," or good data point, for example). These notes will be helpful when you prepare for a class discussion of the article, when you look for quotations from the article for an essay you're writing, or when you begin studying for a quiz or exam that includes information from the reading.

### WRITING ACTIVITY ✦ Using outlining as an on-ramp

Create an outline in the margins of an article you have been assigned to read. See chapter 15 for readings you can practice with.

## 6g One additional strategy: Converse with a reading

When you read actively, you imagine that you are in a conversation with the author. You're not just noting the main ideas, but responding to them—sometimes politely and sometimes with passion, but always respectfully, no matter how you feel about the topic. Conversing with a text involves understanding the text, asking questions, calling attention to ideas that don't make sense, and beginning to draw your own conclusions.

A double-entry notebook can help you to have an academic conversation with a text and its author. On one side of the notebook page, write words, phrases, or sentences from the original text. On the other side of the page, list your questions about, your conclusions about, and your challenges to what you've read. Consider the following brief excerpt from Barbara Ehrenreich's *Bright-sided*, a book in which the experienced journalist questions the power of positive thinking:

> **Americans are a "positive" people. This is our reputation as well as our self-image. We smile a lot and are often baffled when people from other cultures do not return the favor. In the well-worn stereotype, we are upbeat, cheerful, optimistic, and shallow, while foreigners are likely to be subtle, world-weary, and possibly decadent. American expatriate writers like Henry James and James Baldwin wrestled with and occasionally reinforced this stereotype, which I once encountered in the 1980s in the form of a remark by Soviet émigré poet Joseph Brodsky to the effect that the problem with Americans is that they have "never known suffering." (Apparently he didn't know who had invented the blues.) Whether we Americans see it as an embarrassment or a point of pride, being positive—in affect, in mood, in outlook—seems to be engrained in our national character.**
>
> *Source*: Ehrenreich, Barbara. *Bright-sided: How the Relentless Promotion of Positive Thinking Has Undermined America*, Henry Holt, 2009, p. 1.

Here is a sample double-entry notebook page about Ehrenreich's passage.

| *Ideas from the text* | *My responses/questions* |
|---|---|
| "Americans are a 'positive' people. . . . In the well-worn stereotype, we are upbeat, cheerful . . ." (1). | The author puts quotation marks around "positive" and uses the phrase "well-worn stereotype," which makes me think she actually doesn't think we're positive or that she doesn't value positivity. |
| "Whether we Americans see it as an embarrassment or a point of pride, being positive . . . seems to be engrained in our national character" (1). | The author seems to be restating the stereotype but also hinting that there is some debate about it—an interesting idea. It could hint at some disagreement about how we see ourselves or how we want to be seen by others. |

## WRITING ACTIVITY ✦ Using conversing as an on-ramp

Create three or four notebook entries in which you talk back to the author of an assigned reading. See pages 154–155 for an article you can practice with.

# CHAPTER 7

# Strengthening peer review and collaboration skills

With academic writing tasks—or almost any writing task—you should never feel like you have to go it alone. Your peers can provide ideas and insights that you may not have considered. In college and beyond, your writing will benefit as you work with others, either through peer review or by collaborating on a project. During peer review, you will share your work with others, gather their feedback, and use it to revise your writing. You might also review your peers' work and help them improve their drafts. Alternately, you may complete a collaborative assignment, working with others from the start to complete a project. Working with others requires you to communicate well, plan ahead, and be open to new ideas. This chapter offers tips for how to work with others effectively, either during peer review or while collaborating on a project.

## 7a What is peer review?

It's often hard to catch gaps and weaknesses in your own writing. To supplement comments from your instructor, you might ask classmates, friends, colleagues, or writing tutors to review a draft and offer feedback—in other words, to offer a peer review of your work. Other people can help you see your paper differently by pointing out aspects of a draft that are confusing, unclear, or otherwise not working. Your professor may ask you to do peer review in class, or you and your peers may review each other's work on your own. Even though peer review is a social process, it doesn't always happen face to face. File sharing and video chat technologies (think Google Docs and Hangouts, Skype, Zoom, Facetime) can offer productive ways to seek and deliver feedback.

**WRITING ACTIVITY ✦ Your experience with peer review**

Think of a time when someone—a classmate, friend, or other reviewer—gave feedback on your writing that was particularly helpful. Do you remember the feedback? Why do you think it was so helpful? How did you change your writing based on their comments?

## 7b Tips for offering feedback to a peer

The tips below will help you provide useful, constructive feedback when reviewing a peer's writing.

- **Understand the assignment.** Before you begin, make sure you understand what the writer is trying to achieve with a draft. Ask them to describe the assignment and any requirements, their purpose or reason for writing, and what they hope the audience will take from the draft.

- **Focus on global issues.** Give feedback tied to the writer's overall purpose for the project instead of sentence-level mistakes. Instead of correcting grammar, word choice, or spelling, think about the project's big picture: Is the writer's purpose clear? Do you understand their argument? Do their points back up their thesis? Is the essay organized in a way that makes sense?

- **Be organized and strategic.** After you read a draft for the first time, organize your thoughts to guide your feedback. Try identifying the writer's purpose and listing out the points they make to see if their argument is clear. Pinpoint a few aspects of their draft that are particularly effective and a few that need the most improvement. Remember, you are not an editor; avoid proofreading the essay or correcting grammar as you read.

✧ **Think of yourself as a coach, not a judge.** Think of the peer review session as a conversation. Ask questions, offer suggestions, and let the writer decide how to use your advice.

NO *You should rewrite this paragraph to say ___________.*

YES *Try reorganizing this paragraph to make your point clearer.*

✧ **Be constructive.** Although you are focusing on big picture issues, your feedback should be clear, specific, and constructive. Try using *I* statements to explain what you think and following it with your reasoning so that the writer understands why you felt that way. Or give a specific suggestion if you have one, keeping in mind that you should coach them and not dictate changes.

NO *Your conclusion is confusing.*

YES *I was confused by your conclusion because ___________.*

YES *Consider rewriting your conclusion so that it connects back to your thesis.*

### WRITING ACTIVITY ✦ Giving peer review comments

Imagine that Jennifer, the writer of the rough draft you'll see below, has come to you for advice about revising this short essay. What will you tell her? Write your feedback in the margins of her paper and/or on the lines on the next page. Remember to focus on global issues (argument, organization, appeals), not grammar or punctuation, which Jennifer plans to correct after her global revisions.

**Do you care about the planet? If so, there are three important things you can do to reduce your carbon footprint. We use too much carbon, and it is harming Earth. Using less carbon can save the earth and it can save humanitys future.**

**Carbon is an element and it is released by many things such as coal and gasoline. The first thing you can do to use less carbon is use less electricity. Don't forget to turn off your lights and unplug your devices when you leave the house! Try using a fan in the summer instead of running the AC all day. This makes your carbon footprint smaller.**

The second thing you can do is ride a bike or walk. Bikes are pretty cheap and available at almost any sporting goods store. Biking and walking are great forms of exercise so if you bike and walk more you will get fit and look great. If you are going somewhere that's to far to bike or walk, take public transportation instead. The point is to drive less because driving uses gasoline, which releases lots of carbon. Carbon harms the planet by raising its temperature, and humans are speeding up the process by using so much carbon. If you live in a place with no public transportation, get a hybrid or electric car.

It might seem like making a few small changes won't help the planet much. But if everyone did these small things, we could use so much less carbon, that would make Earth a much better place to be. It would make the planet healthier and it would be around for our grandchildren and their grandchildren. Reducing your carbon footprint will help everyone.

______________________________________________

______________________________________________

______________________________________________

______________________________________________

______________________________________________

## 7c Tips for working with feedback from a peer

While feedback from your peers is helpful, you might have trouble making decisions about how to work (or whether to work) suggestions into your writing. The following tips will help you use peer comments to revise your draft effectively.

- **Guide your reviewers.** Explain the assignment, your purpose for writing, and some background on your topic. If you have specific concerns, let your reviewers know. Try starting them off with a few questions you have to let them know where to start. ("Have I organized my argument so it's easy to follow?" "In this paragraph, I want to make the point that ___________. Is that point clear?")
- **Treat peer review as a conversation.** Once you have feedback, ask questions about comments that confuse you. If a reviewer gives feedback that's too general, ask

why they feel that way, or to point to examples in your paper. You may even want to run changes by your reviewers to see if you've addressed their concerns.

- **Be open.** When someone criticizes your writing, it's easy to get defensive. Remember that their feedback is meant to help you, not attack you or your paper. Instead of taking negative feedback personally, consider why readers feel that way and what you can change to address their concerns. This more positive attitude will help you become a better writer.
- **Weigh your feedback.** If you have comments from multiple reviewers, you may be faced with more changes than you can realistically make, or even comments that conflict with each other. As you sort through feedback, keep your draft's purpose in mind. Focus on comments that best help you reach your goals for the assignment. Don't feel obligated to address or agree with every comment, as long as you consider them fairly.

## 7d What is collaboration?

As a college writer, you may work together, or collaborate, on a project with a partner or group. Instead of writing on your own and then gathering your peers' feedback, you will need to work with others through every step of the process—brainstorming, researching, drafting, and revising. Collaborative work gives you an opportunity to explore new ideas and communicate with others about a project. It's also valuable practice for work you will do outside of school. Many professional projects are done in teams.

### WRITING ACTIVITY ✦ Your experiences with collaboration

Think about the last time you worked with others to complete a report, presentation, or other group project. How was the process different from working on a project on your own? What worked well, and what didn't?

## 7e Tips for collaborating effectively

While working with a group can make a project stronger, collaborating effectively takes practice. Below are a few tips for working with others.

- **Organize yourselves, and stay on task.** Functioning well as a group means checking in often and planning together. Although the bulk of the work on a project might be done online, finding ways to meet and communicate as a group will help you stay on track. Here are three ways to keep focused and make progress:

  1. Set up specific meeting times
  2. Assign someone to take notes when you meet as a group (an ongoing Google doc works well for this)
  3. Make sure everyone knows who's doing what for the project

- **Do the work together, and learn from each other.** Resist the urge to just divvy up tasks (one person does the research, another does the writing, another designs the final document and adds citations), even though this method can be convenient. Managing a project like this can result in work that looks like a FrankenProject—lots of pieces stitched together into a monstrous, messy whole. If you work together on every aspect of the project, you will have a stronger, more coherent final product. This method will also allow you and your team members to learn from one another.

- **Communicate and compromise.** Include everyone in conversations and plans for the project. Brainstorm as a group, discuss all of your options, and ask other group members for their opinions. You and your peers may not always agree, but that's a good thing: Debating ideas and hearing multiple perspectives will strengthen your final project. Remember to be open-minded, respectful, and willing to compromise.

- **Know your own strengths, and be ready to admit your weaknesses.** One way to start, especially if you're working with classmates you don't know well, is to think about how you typically like to work in a team or a group. What are you good at? What do you need to improve? Knowing who is best at what can help you assign roles and divide work effectively.

## Assess your strengths as a collaborator

Your responses to the questionnaire below can help you and your group members get to know each other and start a conversation about how to move forward on your project.

| | | | |
|---|---|---|---|
| I am good at being a **team organizer.** | yes | no | kind of |
| I am good at being a **team member.** | yes | no | kind of |
| I am good at **communication** (asking good questions, facilitating discussions, and emailing the instructor). | yes | no | kind of |
| I am good at thinking about the **big picture** (staying focused on the main idea or goal of the project). | yes | no | kind of |
| I am good at thinking about **small details** (completing individual tasks and keeping track of smaller parts of the project). | yes | no | kind of |
| I am good at doing **research** (performing web searches, gathering information from library databases, and conducting surveys or interviews with people). | yes | no | kind of |
| I am good at **design** work (working with or creating images, or thinking about layouts and color schemes). | yes | no | kind of |
| I am good at **writing** (brainstorming, drafting, and editing written materials). | yes | no | kind of |
| I have good **technology** skills (creating basic web pages, making slide show presentations, and working with video). | yes | no | kind of |

# CHAPTER 8

# Outlining and planning your writing

Creating an informal or formal outline early in your process can help you plan your writing clearly and logically. Outlines are useful in allowing you to see your organization at a glance and identify parts of the essay that might need additional evidence.

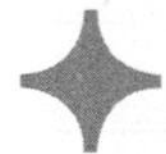

## 8a Use an informal outline to plan

An informal outline can be as simple as the thesis (or working thesis) followed by a list of major ideas.

**SAMPLE INFORMAL OUTLINE**

**Kindergarten is becoming too focused on academics instead of play.**

- **Early reading skills are emphasized, often at the expense of arts and music.**
- **Teacher effectiveness is measured through test scores, encouraging more testing more often.**
- **Less time for recess means less learning through free play.**
- **Kids are expected to sit still and listen for longer stretches of time.**
- **Crucial social, emotional, and physical skills are being neglected in favor of academic lessons.**

Once you have a list of ideas, turn it into a rough outline by deleting some ideas, adding others, and putting the ideas in a logical order.

**WRITING ACTIVITY** ✦ Create an informal outline for your own topic.

Working thesis: ____________________

____________________

- ____________________

  ____________________

- ____________________

  ____________________

- ____________________

  ____________________

- ____________________

  ____________________

- ____________________

  ____________________

- ____________________

  ____________________

It can be helpful to review your outline and think about how this piece of writing might take shape. Reflect on both your *opportunities* and your *challenges* in developing an essay from this outline. You can also start to plan your next steps, working toward your final due date.

What are the strongest supporting points, details, or pieces of evidence in the essay?

____________________

____________________

____________________

About which part of the outline do you feel most confident? ____________

______________________________________________

______________________________________________

Which parts of the outline need to be strengthened? ____________

______________________________________________

______________________________________________

What resources can provide the necessary additional information? ____________

______________________________________________

______________________________________________

## 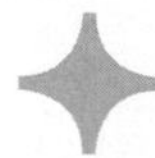 8b Use a formal outline to plan

Early in the writing process, informal outlines have certain advantages: They can be drafted quickly and revised easily. Especially for complex topics, though, a formal outline may be useful later on, after you have written a rough draft. A formal outline can help you see whether your essay is structured logically and whether each part has enough supporting evidence.

Take a look at the following formal outline. Notice that the student's thesis is the basis of the outline; everything else in the outline supports that thesis. This outline specifies both major points that directly support the thesis (I, II, III) and minor points that flesh out the major points (A, B, C).

**SAMPLE FORMAL OUTLINE**

**Thesis: Given technological advances and our "on-demand" culture, states should implement same-day voter registration.**

**I. Same-day registration will increase voter turnout.**

**A. Low voter participation is a serious problem across the country, especially among youth, minorities, low-income populations, and people with disabilities.**

B. **Eligible citizens may be turned away at the polls because they have not planned ahead and registered two to four weeks in advance.**

C. **Same-day registration would enable people to vote even if they move out of state just before the election.**

II. **Voting is a right established by the Constitution, and protecting voting rights is essential to our democracy.**

A. **Eligible voters should not be prohibited from voting because of arbitrary early registration deadlines.**

B. **Currently, states may "purge" from their rolls eligible voters who have not voted in several recent elections. Skipping past elections should not disqualify voters from voting in future elections.**

III. **Same-day registration modernizes and simplifies the voting process.**

A. **Just like absentee ballots, electronic voting, and early voting periods, same-day registration is one more resource that makes voting more convenient.**

B. **As we have modernized other civic systems to be more convenient, such as paying tolls or obtaining driver's licenses, same-day registration makes voting more convenient and requires fewer resources than early voting periods.**

C. **Same-day voter registration would allow voters' registrations to accompany them any time they move.**

In drafting a formal outline, keep the following guidelines in mind.

1. Start with your working thesis at the top of the outline. Reread it often to remind yourself what you are trying to convey
2. Make major points (I, II, III) and minor points (A, B, C) as parallel as possible.
3. Use complete sentences, unless phrases are clear.
4. Use the conventional system of numbers and letters to designate levels.

   I.

   A.

   B.

1.

2.

a.

b.

5. Check that you have more than one point for each level. If you are going to go to the next level, be sure you have at least two sub-points to support the point you are making.

6. Be flexible. You will likely need to revise your outline as your draft evolves.

**WRITING ACTIVITY** ✦ Use one of the two templates below to create a formal outline for your own topic. Here is an outline template with two levels of support.

Thesis statement: ______________________________

______________________________

______________________________

I. ______________________________

______________________________

A. ______________________________

______________________________

B. ______________________________

______________________________

C. ______________________________

______________________________

II. ______________________________

______________________________

A. ______________________________

______________________________

B. ______________________________

______________________________

C. ______________________________

______________________________

III. ______________________________

______________________________

A. ______________________________

______________________________

B. ______________________________

______________________________

C. ______________________________

______________________________

Here is an outline template with three levels of support. You can use the numbered levels (1, 2, 3) to identify the evidence that will support your earlier points.

Thesis statement: ______________________________

______________________________

______________________________

I. ______________________________

______________________________

A. ______________________________

______________________________

1. ______________________________

______________________________

2. ______________________________

______________________________

B. ______________________________

______________________________

1. ______________________________

______________________________

2. ______________________________

______________________________

C. ______________________________

______________________________

1. ______________________________

______________________________

2. ______________________________

______________________________

II. ______________________________

______________________________

A. ______________________________

______________________________

1. ______________________________

______________________________

2. ______________________________

______________________________

B. ______________________________

______________________________

1. ______________________________

______________________________

2. ______________________________

______________________________

C. ______________________________

______________________________

1. ______________________________

______________________________

2. ______________________________

______________________________

III. ______________________________________________

______________________________________________

A. ______________________________________________

______________________________________________

1. ______________________________________________

______________________________________________

2. ______________________________________________

______________________________________________

B. ______________________________________________

______________________________________________

1. ______________________________________________

______________________________________________

2. ______________________________________________

______________________________________________

C. ______________________________________________

______________________________________________

1. ______________________________________________

______________________________________________

## 8c Use headings to plan

Many writers of essays, reports, or professional documents use headings to break up a long piece of writing into clear sections. Headings can also help your readers follow the organization of your document. Use headings as a planning device as you draft, grouping your essay into relevant sections and inserting a topical heading for each section of text. Experiment with a few different groupings to suit your purpose and audience.

One student decided to use headings to group her ideas about microplastics in the oceans. She did some initial research about the topic, then she wrote her first draft exploring the issues she learned about. She tried to envision the organization that would best help her readers to understand the issue. Here are the headings she used to group parts of her essay.

The problem of plastic pollution (introduction)

Cause: single-use plastic consumer goods

Cause: low rates of recycling

Effects of microplastics on sea life

Effects of microplastics on human life

Potential solutions: individual efforts vs. legislation

Call to action

##  8d Use a map to plan

Outlines are helpful for organizing your ideas, but if you are a visual learner, mapping or clustering may work better. Clustering loosely arranges ideas to show how they are connected. Mapping emphasizes both relationships among ideas and the hierarchy, or different levels, of your points and subpoints.

For example, in the diagram on the following page, suppose that each circle contains an idea or piece of evidence. The circle at the top represents the major point or claim. Three supporting points support that claim, and finally several sub-points provide further details or evidence.

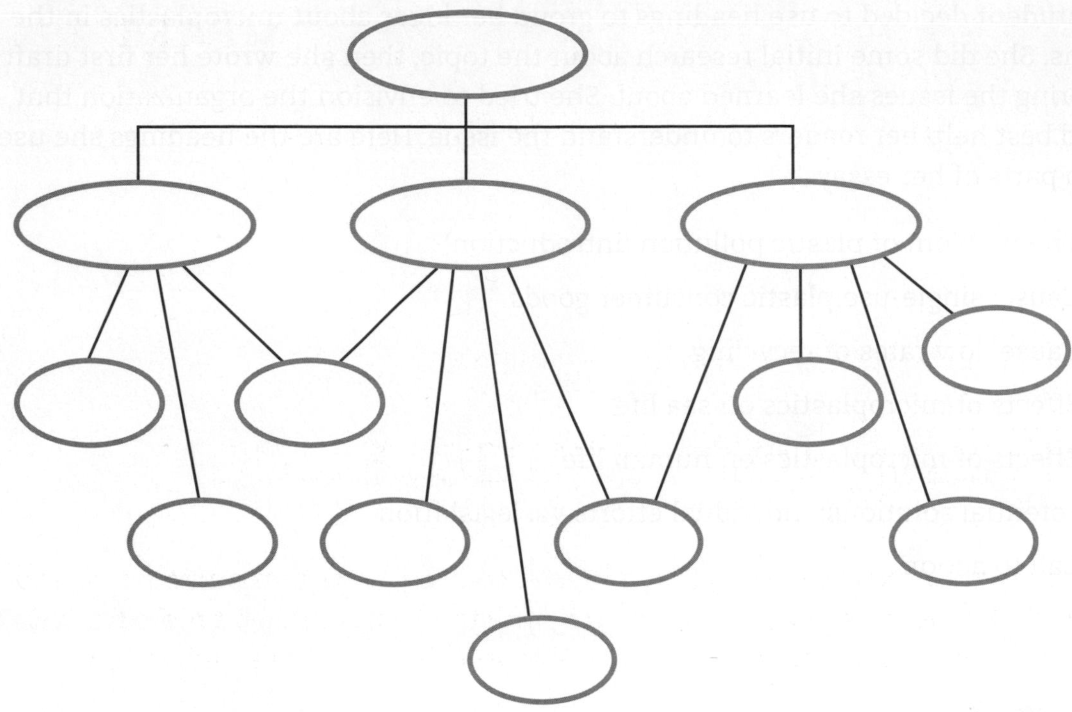

You can create a simple cluster by writing your main topic or claim in the middle of a blank page. Then, think of all the subtopics or sub-points related to that main idea. Some possibilities include causes, effects, advantages, disadvantages, reasons, or supporting evidence. Make a circle for each one, and draw lines or arrows connecting the subtopics to your central one. Keep extending the cluster as needed. Putting your ideas into a graphic form like this can help you think through what you want to say in your essay.

# CHAPTER 9

# Writing for an audience

When you write academic essays, do you ever consider who your audience is? You might think that you are writing for your instructors, but think a bit more flexibly. It's likely that they aren't your only audience—especially if you are creating digital writing.

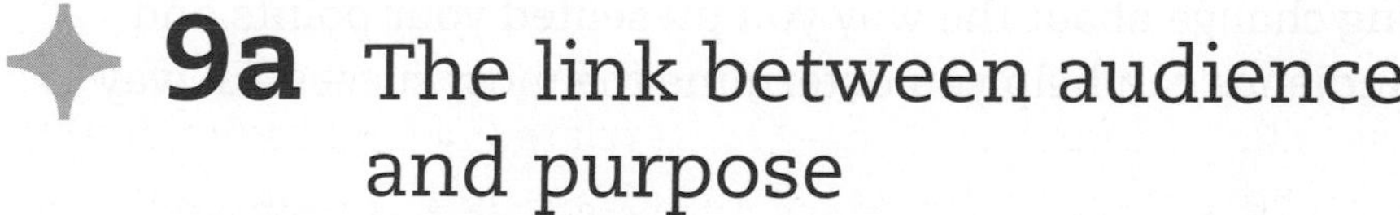

## 9a The link between audience and purpose

All successful writing needs to demonstrate audience awareness. At its most basic level, audience awareness means paying attention to the person or group that will read, hear, or view your writing or the person or group to whom you are making an appeal. Audiences have needs and expectations related to your writing, and those needs and expectations may vary from audience to audience. This means that audience and purpose (why you are writing to or communicating with that audience) are closely linked.

In many cases, your teacher will read and grade your writing. So what are your teacher's needs and expectations regarding your essay or project? Regardless of the subject, your writing should show that you are knowledgeable and thoughtful about the subject, can communicate your ideas clearly, and can write in grammatically accurate, error-free sentences. Those are expectations that all teachers will have, in addition to any expectations related to specific requirements or guidelines for the assignment.

If, like many composition courses, your class involves peer review workshops, in which one or more classmates will review your essay and offer feedback, then your teacher is not your only audience. You can consider your peers (classmates) to be part of your audience as well. Finally, if your assignment invites you to post part or all of your project online, your audience is likely to be larger and less predictable than you might have assumed.

##  9b Specific and specialized audiences

You may be asked to address a *target audience*, a specific group of readers whose characteristics will affect what you write and how you write it. For example, some professors ask students to write on the same subject to two different audiences to show how audience affects their essay. Imagine writing an essay in which you argue that your state should ban smoking in all public spaces; imagine addressing your argument to a group of nonsmokers. Then imagine that your instructor assigned you to argue for the same ban but to address smokers. Your purpose or reason for writing would be the same, but your readers would differ. Would you make the same arguments? Would anything change about the way you presented your points and evidence? Knowing your audience can help you determine the most successful way to write your essay.

A *specialized audience*, one with a certain technical expertise, may require a different approach than a broader audience. For example, you could aim your argument for more regular clean-up of local streams and rivers to a general civic audience, to a target audience of county administrators, or to a specialized audience of environmental scientists.

##  9c Thinking about content, tone, vocabulary, and exigence

Effective audience awareness can influence many different elements of your essay, such as content, tone, vocabulary, and exigence.

**Content** Some readers will need more detail than others. For example, if you were writing about climate change and addressing your classmates (who may or may not have in-depth knowledge of your topic), you might need to include background information to help readers understand the subject. You might need to define terms such as *carbon footprint* or describe a process such as the greenhouse effect. But a more knowledgeable audience (a group of environmental scientists) would not need such background information. In fact, knowledgeable readers may not want you to include information they consider unnecessary; they may perceive it as wasting their time. Conversely, general readers may not appreciate having to navigate unfamiliar technical terms and complex concepts that are not explained.

**Tone** Tone, the attitude or feeling conveyed by the author, will change depending on the audience. When addressing friends, you may choose to use an informal, conversational tone; however, when addressing other scholars, you may adopt a more formal, academic tone. For example, if you were writing about a topic such as human trafficking, you would not want to adopt a casual, light-hearted tone because your readers would assume that you were not serious about your subject.

These two sample sentences contain the same content but communicate different tones. How would you describe the difference?

> **Some foolish people mistakenly feel that climate change is not an important issue, but they are totally wrong, and scientific evidence proves that those people don't know what they're talking about!**
>
> **While some people argue that climate change is not an important issue, there is scientific evidence that strongly suggests that climate change actively affects the environment.**

While both sentences emphasize the importance of climate change, the first has a disrespectful tone; the writer suggests that anyone who disagrees is idiotic. Such a tone is likely to alienate readers who have a different viewpoint. In addition, the use of contractions ("don't," "they're") creates an informal tone that is not usually appropriate for academic essays. The second sentence makes the same point about the importance of climate change, yet maintains a respectful and academic tone. It acknowledges that people can disagree on a subject without resorting to insults. Which one of the two sentences would prompt you to keep reading?

**Vocabulary** Knowledgeable audiences are likely to be comfortable with jargon (technical, subject-specific terms) and can handle elevated diction (the level of formality of words). General readers prefer a lower level of diction and may need to have technical terms defined. While it is likely that a group of college-level biology students would be familiar with terms like *allele* and *cytoplasm*, you could not expect a general audience to understand such terminology without explanation.

**Exigence** Exigence is an urgency or need that must be addressed. It's an opportunity to make something happen. Your goal is to make something happen—whether that means changing or opening someone's mind, explaining or solving a problem, creating action or movement, raising funds or awareness, or something else. To establish exigence in an essay or other writing, you must answer a basic question: Why should your readers care about your topic and your purpose? Your handbook refers to this as the "So what?" test. Why does your topic matter to your readers? Notice that asking this question is different from asking why you yourself care about the topic and purpose. You need to be able to explain why your readers will need or want to know about your subject. The exigence may vary for different members of your audience. For example, if your purpose is to argue for more land to be set aside for state parks, some readers may care passionately about having more green spaces while others may be more concerned about the costs of creating and maintaining park areas. If you can identify what matters to your audience, you can generate interest by addressing those issues.

Once you have pinpointed your target audience, the next step is to develop strategies to identify that audience's key characteristics.

## 9d Questions to help identify audience characteristics

While it is difficult to completely identify your audience (there are many variables, such as culture, age, knowledge level, and beliefs), you can gain a clearer picture by trying to answer some basic questions.

- **What do you already know about your readers?** Can you identify their age range, education level, or expectations for the essay?

- **What is their level of knowledge?** What do readers already know about your topic? What will they need to know in order to understand your purpose and your points? Will they be familiar with technical terms, or will those terms need to be explained?

- **What are your readers' current attitudes toward your topic and purpose?** Will readers generally agree with your point of view or be resistant to your ideas?

- **If you are taking a position on your topic, what weaknesses will readers find in your argument?** Why (and how) might they oppose your viewpoint? What specific arguments might they disagree with? What counterargument might they be able to make to refute your point?

- **What values, beliefs, or assumptions about your topic does your audience hold?** Are there common links between you and your readers? If you can find connections between your own attitudes toward your topic and those of your readers, you can show them how your essay relates to their interests, which can make them much more open to what you have to say.

You may not be able to answer all of these questions fully. Your goal is to make an informed estimate of your audience's characteristics. But the more aware you are of your target audience, the better you will be able to tailor your essay to meet their needs and expectations.

##  9e Comparing sample paragraphs

To illustrate the value of audience awareness in composition, consider the following two paragraphs, both intended to introduce the subject of climate change. Which one seems more appropriate for an academic essay? Why?

**PARAGRAPH 1**

**Some folks say that we don't hurt the planet with our actions. Others think we do. No doubt there's a ton of crazy weather these days, right? Hurricanes, blizzards, tornadoes, floods, giant ocean waves crashing over the coast, and who knows what else. Nature's playing some nasty tricks on us! So we need to get to the bottom of it all and figure out what's causing all this craziness. Are we responsible for climate change or is it just a natural thing that would happen no matter what? I think we must be a least part of the problem because of all the cars we drive and exhaust from factories.**

**PARAGRAPH 2**

**There are conflicting arguments about the cause of climate change in our society. While some people argue that humans are responsible for climate change due to the overuse of resources such as fossil fuels, others argue that any such changes are simply part of the Earth's natural weather cycles. While it is undeniable that extreme weather conditions, such as hurricanes, tornadoes, blizzards, and floods, seem to be more prevalent these days, what is less certain is the cause of these phenomena. While the cause is debatable, there is ample evidence to indicate that humans are at least partly responsible for climate change due to an overreliance on fossil fuels and the resulting carbon emissions.**

Both paragraphs discuss similar ideas; they both provide a general introduction to an ongoing debate about climate change and its causes. But does one paragraph seem more appropriate and effective for its target audience? Paragraph 1 creates an informal tone, uses slang and colloquial vocabulary, and seems more suited for a casual conversation with friends or perhaps a social media post designed to start a conversation. Furthermore, its use of first-person point of view personalizes the argument rather than remaining objective. Paragraph 2 maintains a more formal tone, uses more elevated diction, and more clearly targets an academic audience. The use of third-person point of view helps establish a level of credibility and objectivity appropriate for its subject and audience.

Audience awareness is an essential component of an academic essay or any communication. Accurately identifying your target audience allows you to shape your writing to meet your readers' needs and expectations, creating a better effect overall. When preparing to write, always take the time to ask yourself, "Who are my readers and why am I writing to them?"

### WRITING ACTIVITY ✦ Making adjustments for audience

For each of the following topics, briefly (2–3 sentences) explain how you would adjust tone, content, vocabulary, and exigence to address each listed audience.

1. Do violent video games cause violence in society?
   a. Attendees at a video game convention
   b. Group of concerned parents

______________________________________________

______________________________________________

______________________________________________

______________________________________________

2. A discussion of the effects of climate change
   a. Elementary school students learning about environmental science for the first time
   b. High school science club

______________________________________________

______________________________________________

______________________________________________

______________________________________________

3. The impact of social media
   a. Teenagers who are active on Instagram
   b. School counselors and psychologists

   ______________________________________________

   ______________________________________________

   ______________________________________________

   ______________________________________________

## WRITING ACTIVITY ✦ Crafting an approach to your audience

For each topic listed below, identify a target audience and plan your approach. How would you adjust tone, vocabulary, content, and exigence appropriately? Briefly explain your reasons for your choices.

1. Establishing good study habits in college
   a. Tone: ______________________________________________

   ______________________________________________
   b. Vocabulary: ______________________________________________

   ______________________________________________
   c. Content: ______________________________________________

   ______________________________________________
   d. Exigence: ______________________________________________

   ______________________________________________

2. Preparing to get your driver's license
   a. Tone: ______________________________________________

   ______________________________________________
   b. Vocabulary: ______________________________________________

   ______________________________________________

c. Content: ______________________________

______________________________

d. Exigence: ______________________________

______________________________

3. Conducting a job search after graduation

a. Tone: ______________________________

______________________________

b. Vocabulary: ______________________________

______________________________

c. Content: ______________________________

______________________________

d. Exigence: ______________________________

______________________________

## WRITING ACTIVITY ✦ Revising for audience awareness

Revise the following paragraphs, adjusting the content, tone, vocabulary, and exigence to make the paragraph more appropriate for the stated target audience.

1. Topic: Writing an essay in an English composition course

   Audience: Incoming first-year writers at the college

   **To write an acceptable essay, students will need to exemplify the highest standards of prose. One must exhibit superior grammatical proficiency, superb communicative capability, and a knowledgeable demeanor. In order to produce the most desirable final product, one only need adhere closely to the three most imperative components of the writing process: prewriting (brainstorming), drafting, and revising. One must also be supremely cognizant of the importance**

**of audience awareness. With those facets in mind, students will achieve the maximum anticipated result: a well-crafted, coherent essay.**

2. Topic: Addiction to social media

   Audience: A local organization of parents, youth group leaders, and school officials

   **Social media is a huge problem, you know? There are way too many depressed and stressed out kids in this country, and it's just getting worse with social media. I know this one teen who has been having anxiety attacks because no one likes her posts and she has serious FOMO issues! Everyone knows the problem is getting worse, so what should we do about it? Well, I think we need to help teens and preteens get their act together on Instagram, Twitter, and other platforms. Like, we could give better education on understanding and setting privacy settings and help them block upsetting content or mute a nasty thread! We can do a better job getting teens to think about how social media makes them feel about themselves and others their age. We probably can start making progress with this group!**

# CHAPTER 10

# Graphic organizers for common types of writing

Some students benefit from a visual display of how certain ideas relate to other ideas. Graphic organizers, tools that help students plan their writing by making the relationships between ideas more visually obvious, can be useful for drafting essays and other longer works. The following pages offer graphic organizers for common types of frequently assigned college writing.

# 10a A basic essay

An essay is a piece of writing made up of multiple paragraphs on a single subject. Essays can be informative, persuasive, descriptive, narrative, or some combination of these types. You may be used to the five-paragraph essay formula from high school, but college instructors don't expect you to be so rigid. Some allow a good deal of experimentation depending on the topic, your purpose (reason for writing), and your audience (readers).

## Sample graphic organizer for a basic essay

These boxes are meant to help you organize your thoughts. They do not necessarily represent individual paragraphs.

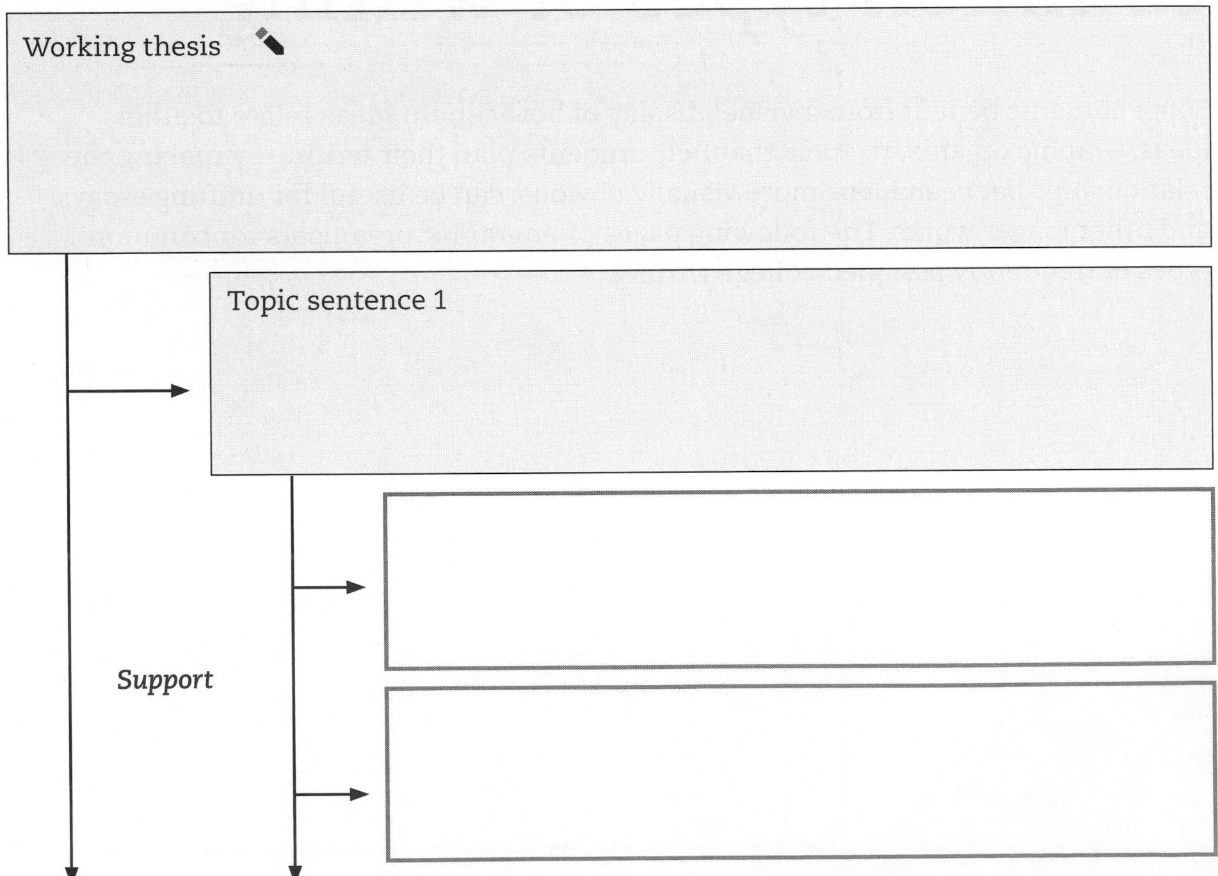

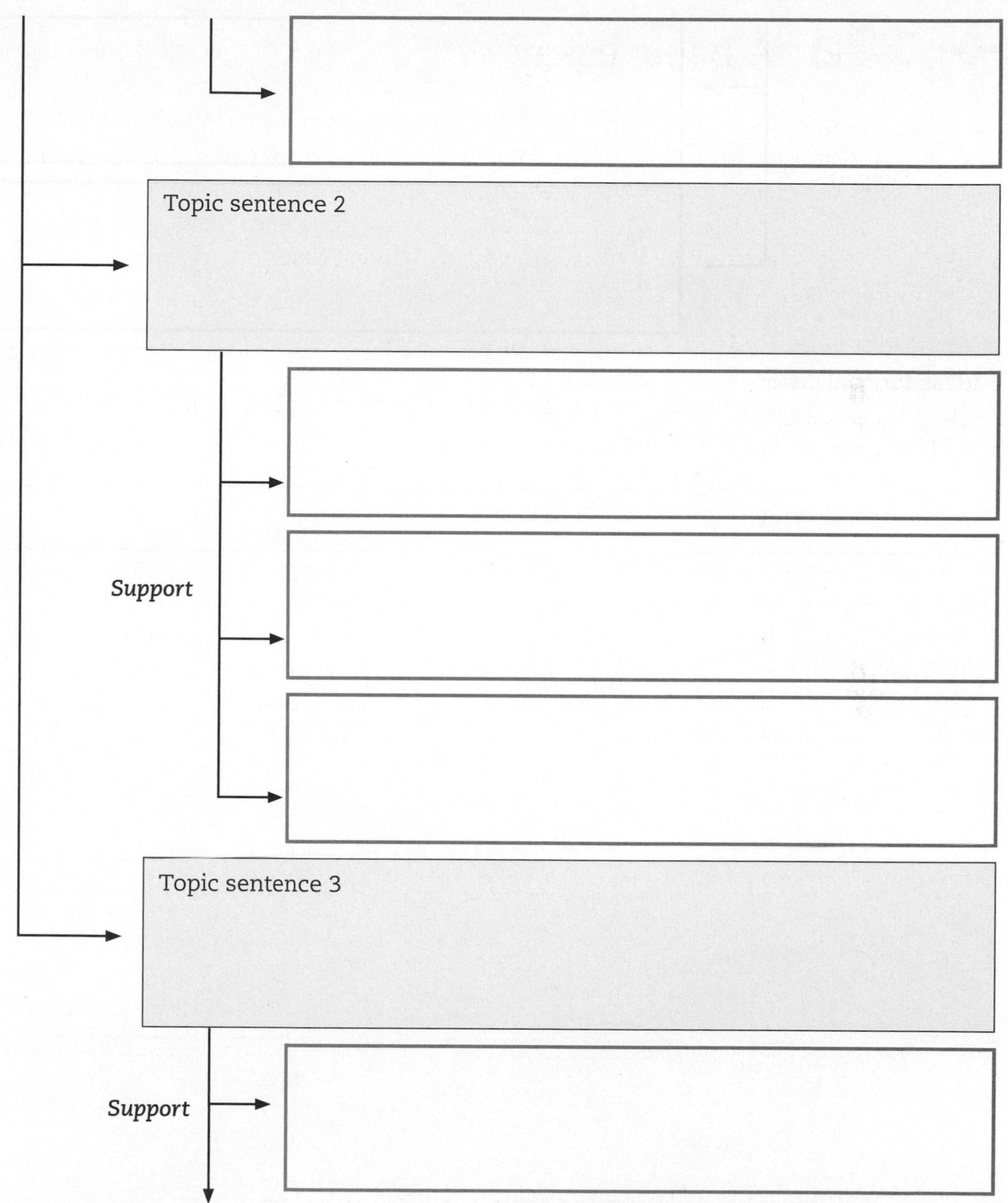
Topic sentence 2
Support
Topic sentence 3
Support

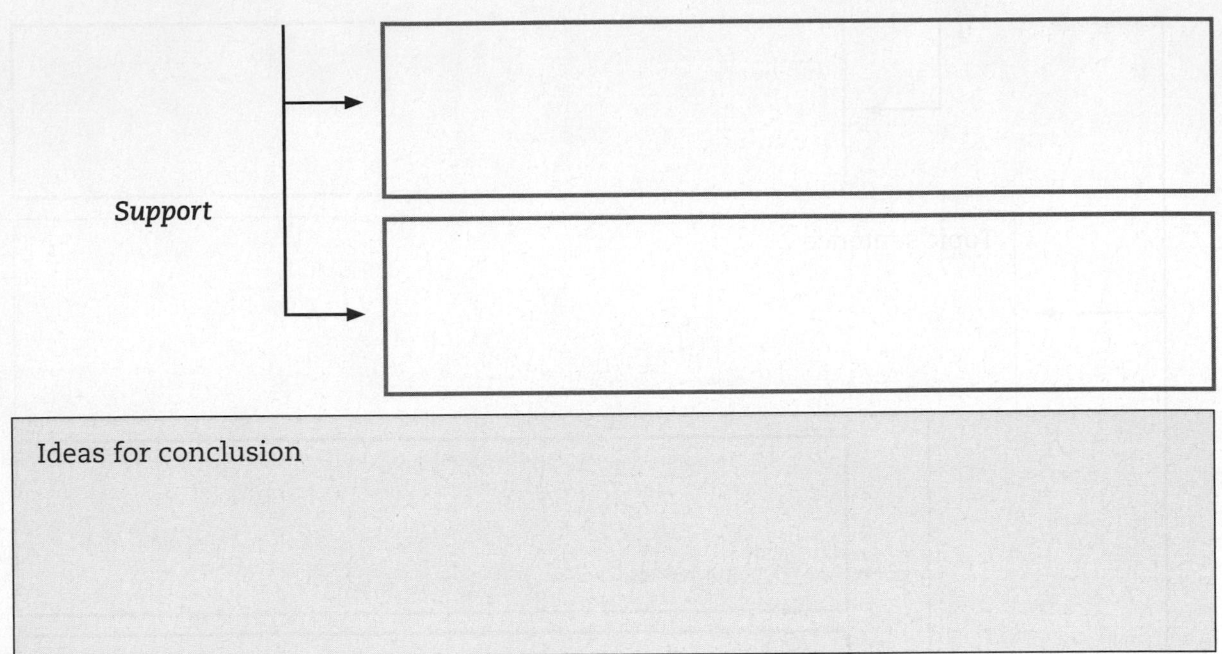
Support
Ideas for conclusion

# 10b An analytical essay

When you analyze something, you break it down to study it, and then you make a judgment about it. If you are writing an analytical essay—about a text, an advertisement, a film, or a work of art—your thesis statement is where you communicate your judgment. The rest of the essay looks at parts of the whole. If you were analyzing a magazine advertisement, your analysis might look at the colors in the ad, the typefaces, and the kinds of appeals used (emotional, logical, and so on), and your ideas about those separate elements would help you form a judgment about how successful the ad was.

## Sample graphic organizer for an analytical essay

These boxes are meant to help you organize your thoughts. They do not necessarily represent individual paragraphs.

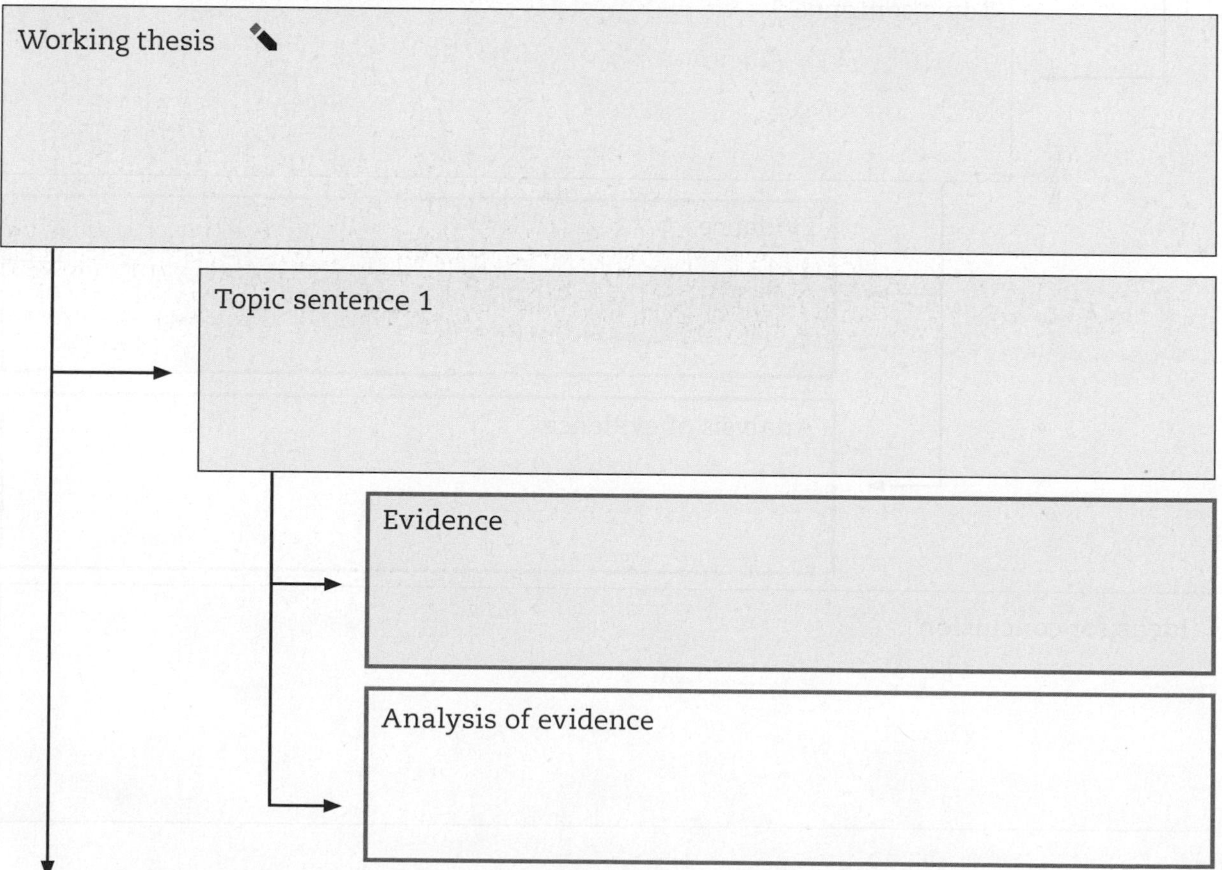

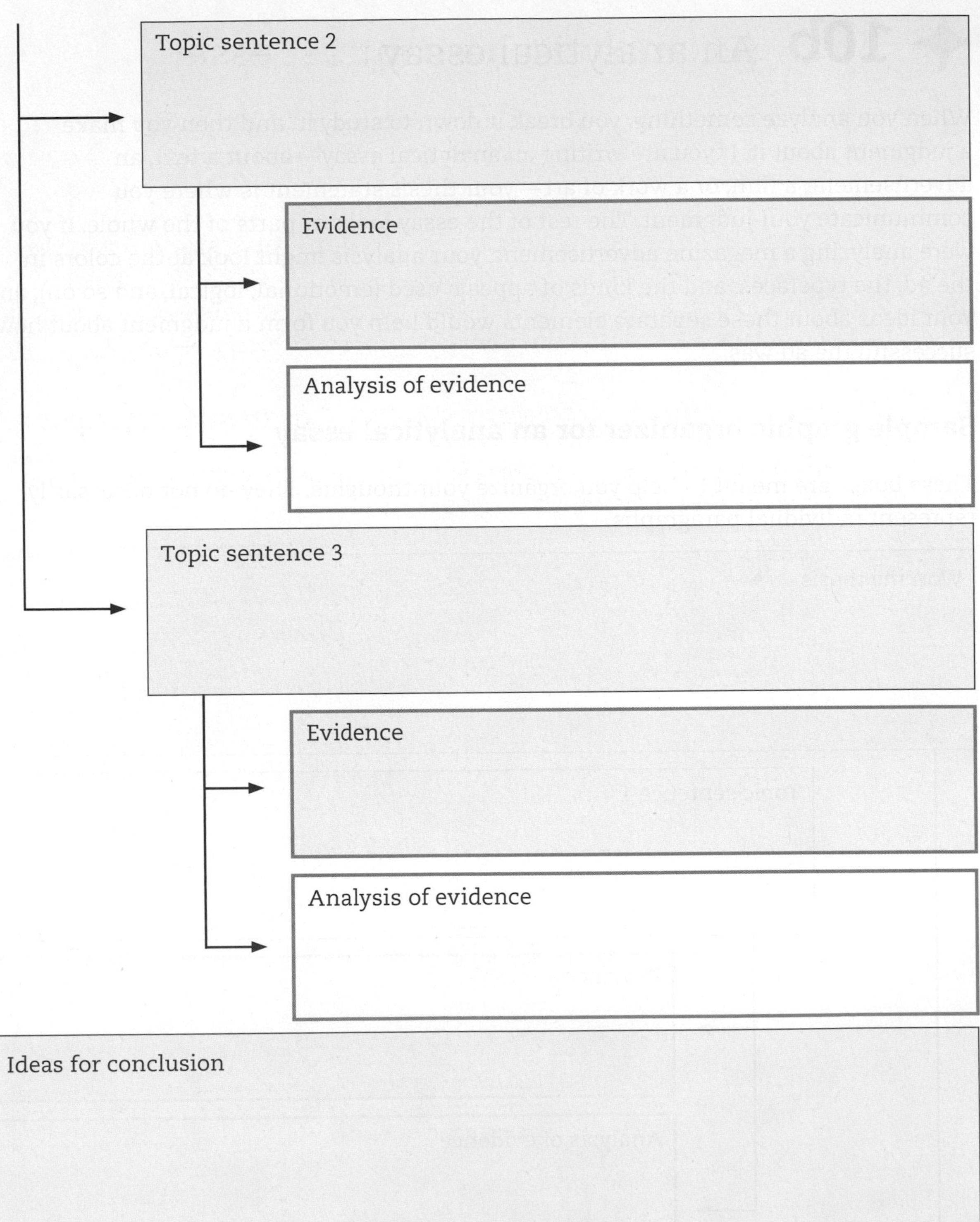
Topic sentence 2
Evidence
Analysis of evidence
Topic sentence 3
Evidence
Analysis of evidence
Ideas for conclusion

# 10c A compare-and-contrast essay

When you compare two people, places, things, or ideas, you draw your readers' attention to the ways in which the two are similar. When you contrast, you write about the ways in which they are different. Often you will be assigned to do both in the same essay.

There are two basic options for organizing a compare-and-contrast essay. You can focus on important features, comparing the two subjects first on one feature and then, one by one, on the others. Or you can start with all the features of one subject and then look at how the second subject compares on all the same features.

## Sample graphic organizer for a compare-and-contrast essay, option 1

These boxes are meant to help you organize your thoughts. They do not necessarily represent individual paragraphs.

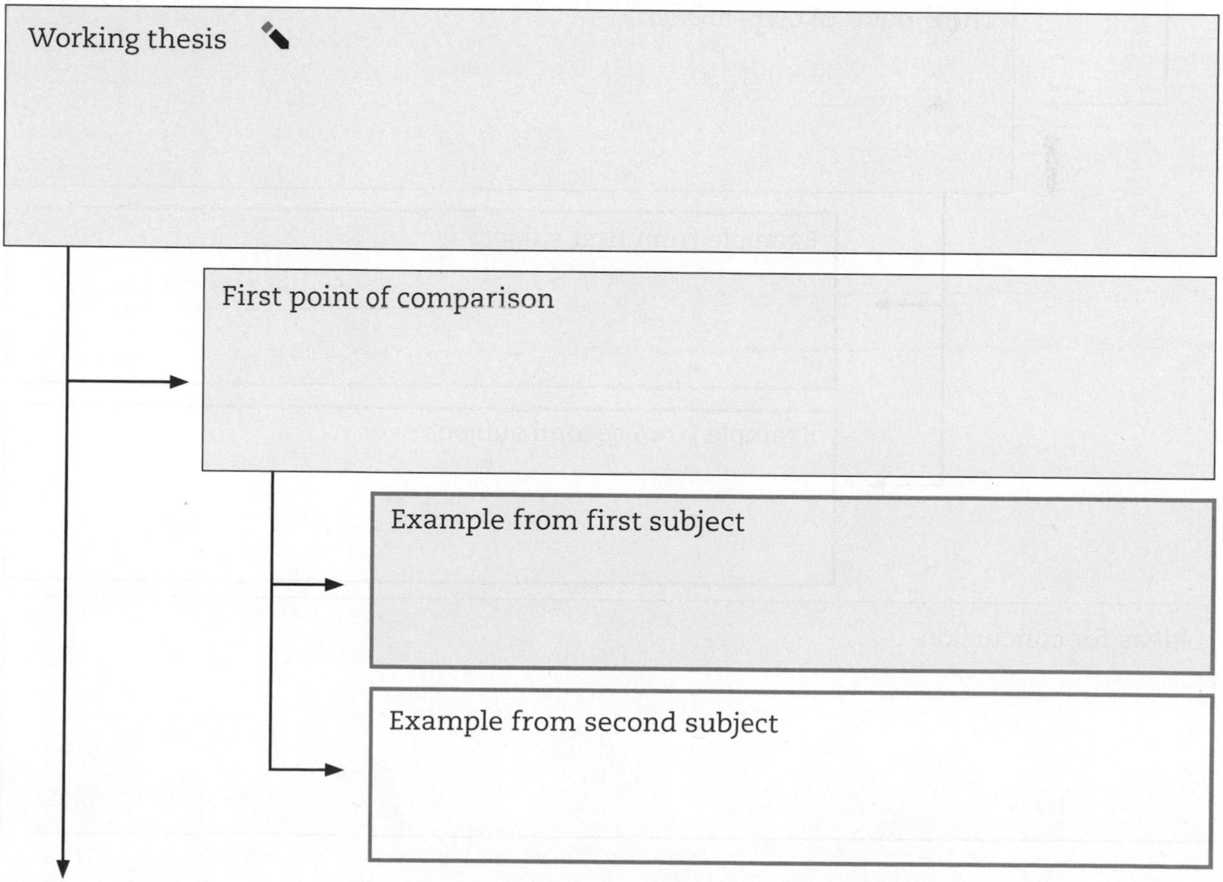

Working thesis

First point of comparison

Example from first subject

Example from second subject

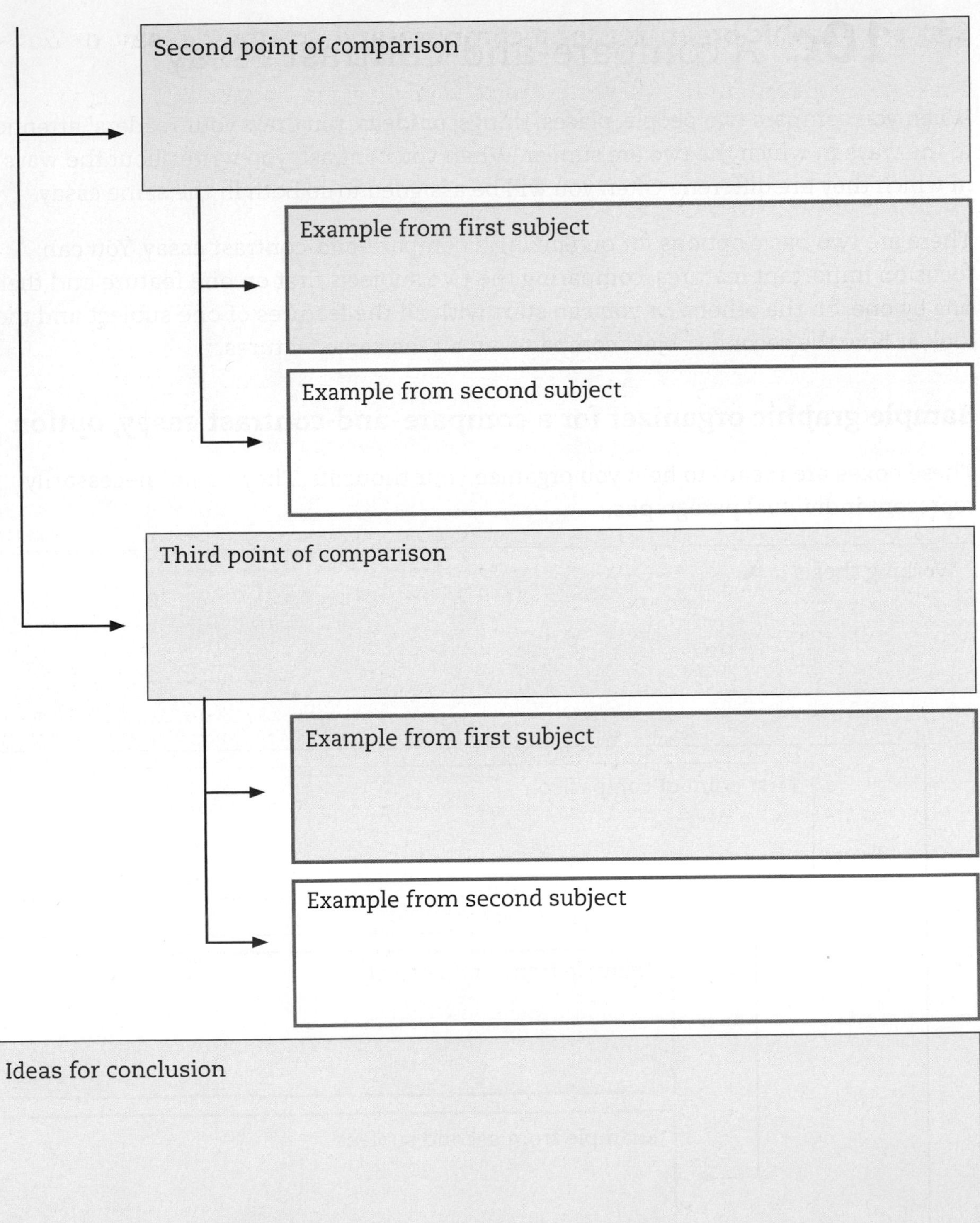
Second point of comparison
Example from first subject
Example from second subject
Third point of comparison
Example from first subject
Example from second subject
Ideas for conclusion

## Sample graphic organizer for a compare-and-contrast essay, option 2

These boxes are meant to help you organize your thoughts. They do not necessarily represent individual paragraphs.

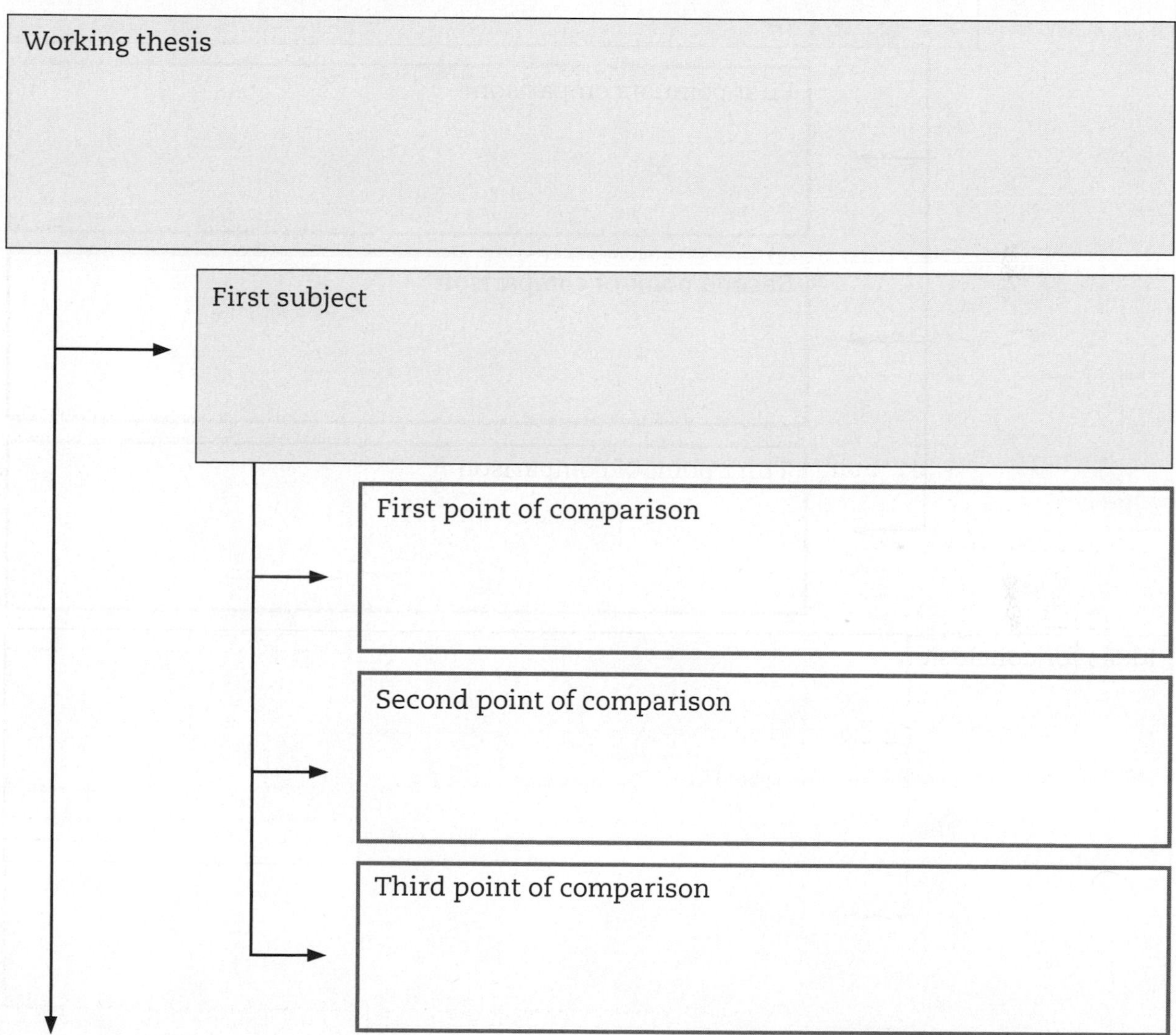

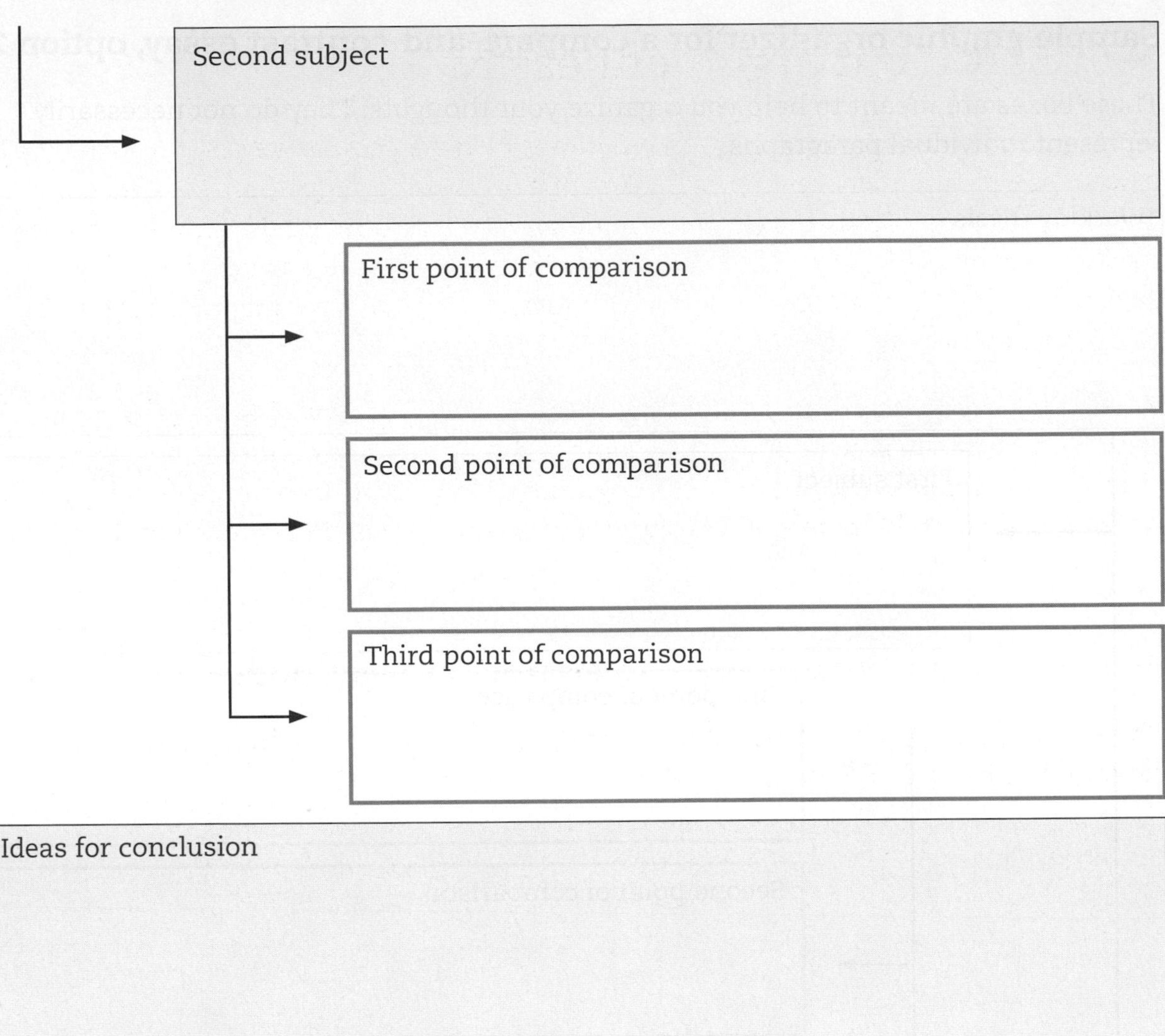
Second subject
First point of comparison
Second point of comparison
Third point of comparison
Ideas for conclusion

# 10d An argument essay

When you write an argument essay, sometimes called a persuasive essay, you set forth a debatable position with evidence; make appeals to emotion (*pathos*), logic (*logos*), and/or credibility (*ethos*); and build common ground. You hope in the end to convince readers to agree with your position or at least consider it to be a valid position. Argument essays for college courses are almost always written using information from one or more sources.

Where and how you address counterarguments—and thus how you organize your argument essay—will depend on your topic and on your argumentative strategy. You may address counterarguments at the beginning of the essay (see option 1), as you work through individual reasons in support of your own position (see option 2), or at the end of the essay.

## Sample graphic organizer for an argument essay, option 1

These boxes are meant to help you organize your thoughts. They do not necessarily represent individual paragraphs.

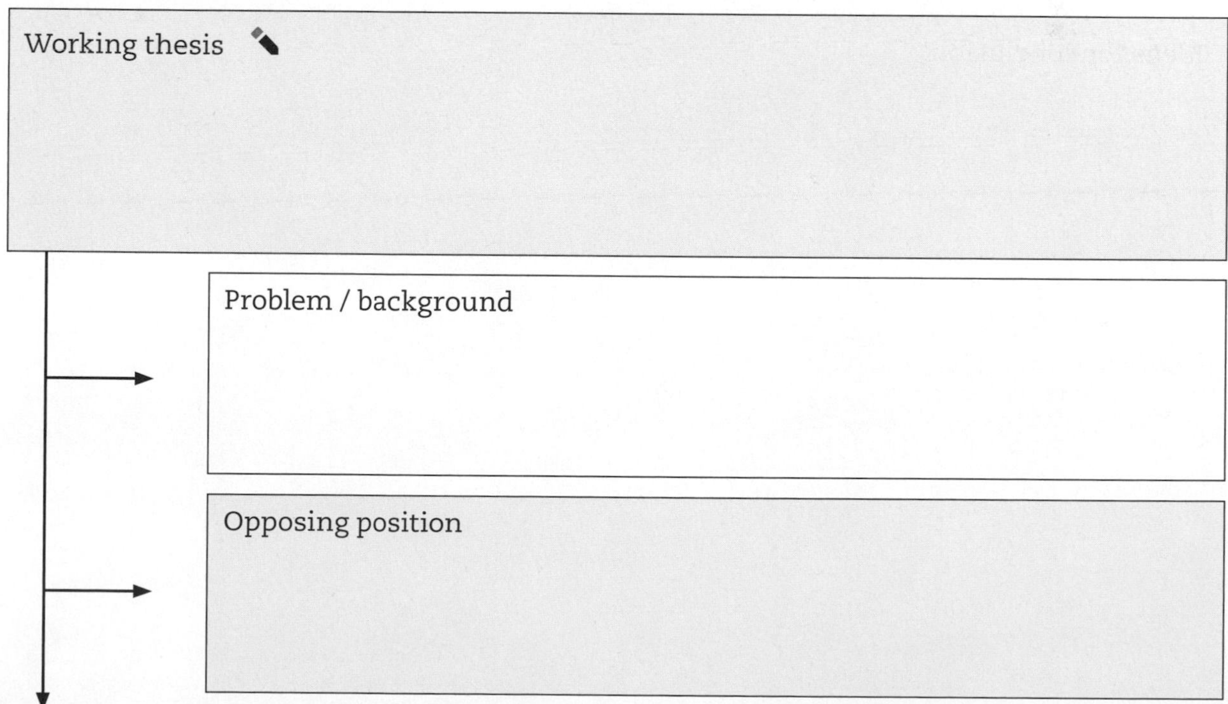

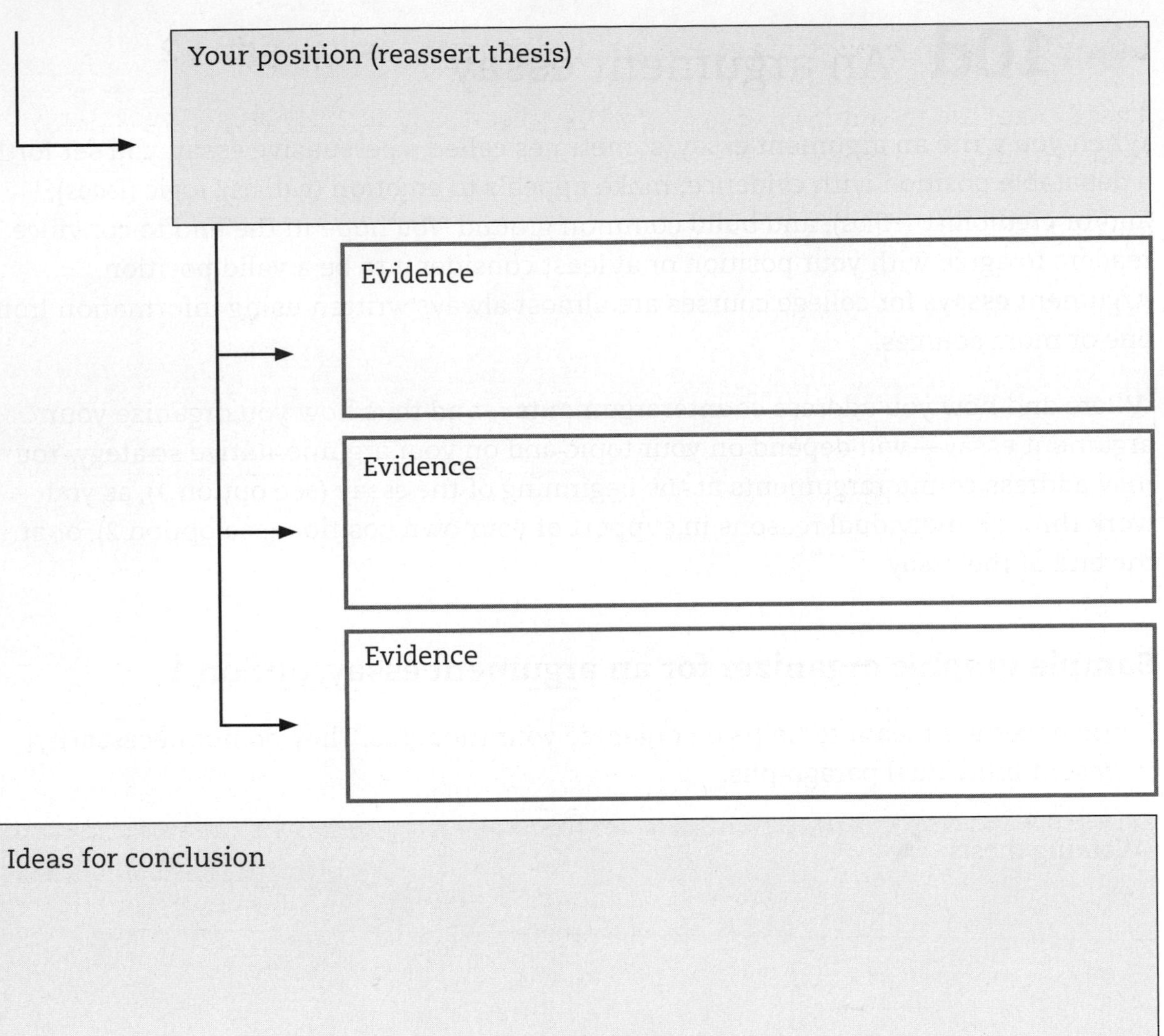
Your position (reassert thesis)
Evidence
Evidence
Evidence
Ideas for conclusion

## Sample graphic organizer for an argument essay, option 2

These boxes are meant to help you organize your thoughts. They do not necessarily represent individual paragraphs.

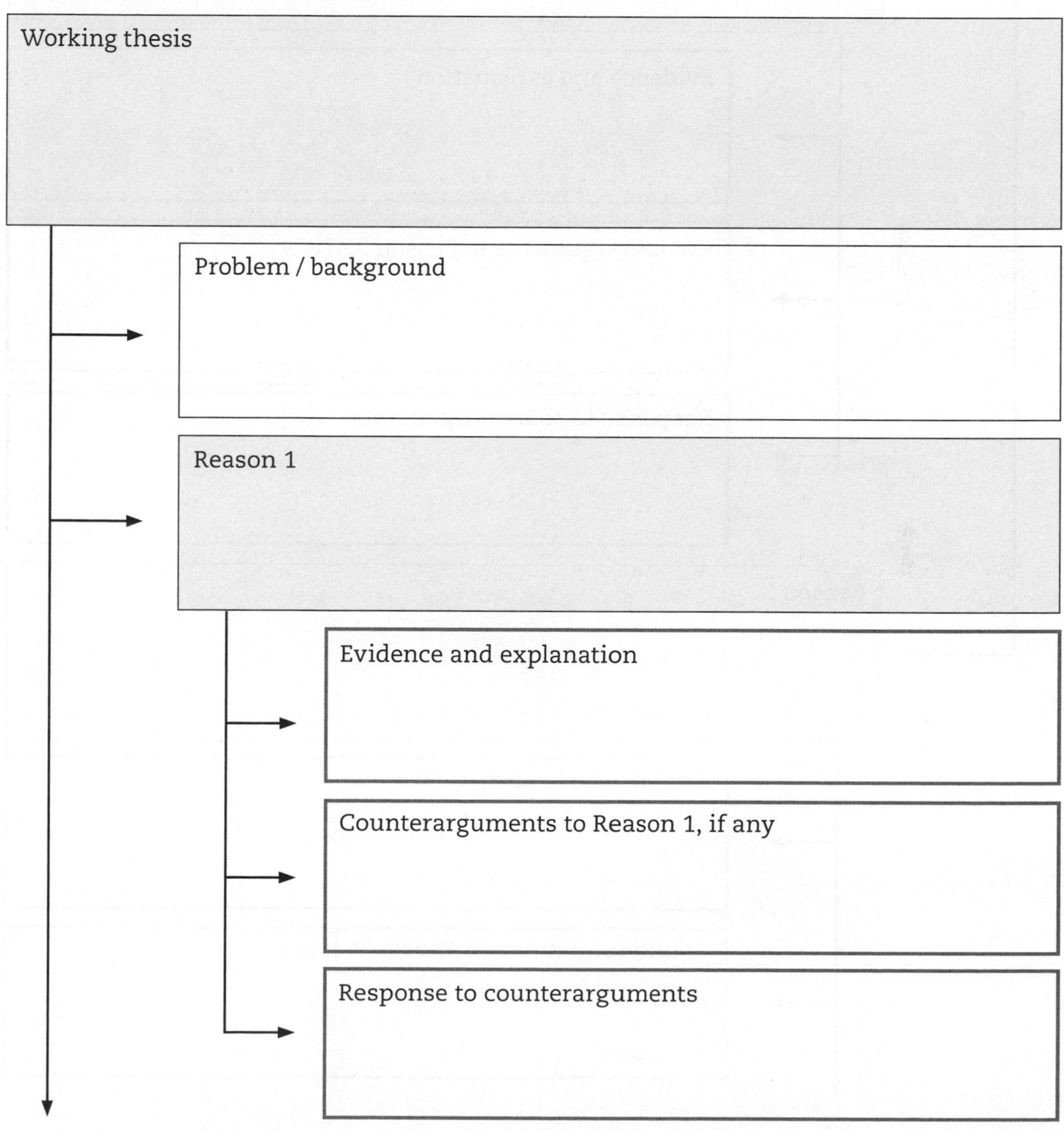

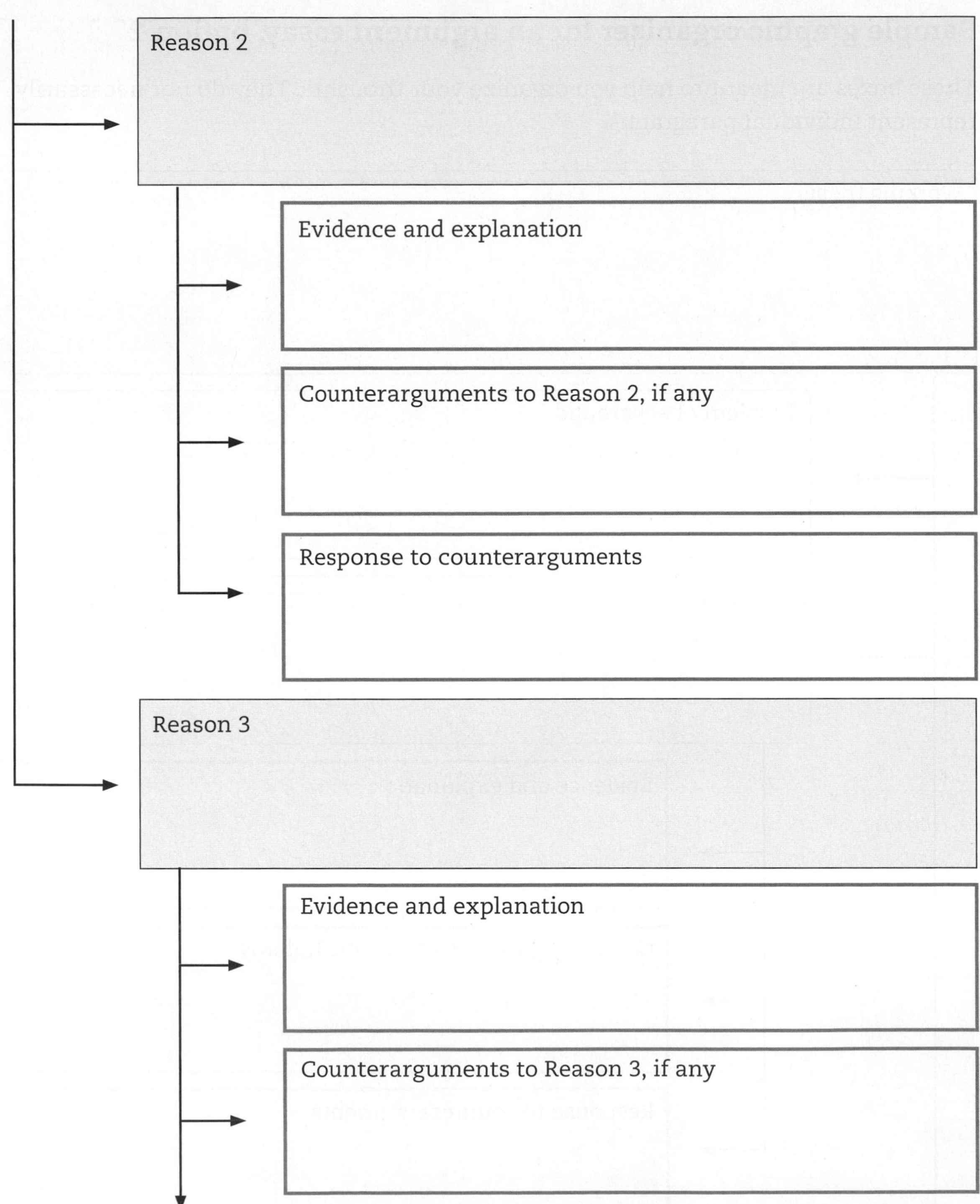
Reason 2
Evidence and explanation
Counterarguments to Reason 2, if any
Response to counterarguments
Reason 3
Evidence and explanation
Counterarguments to Reason 3, if any

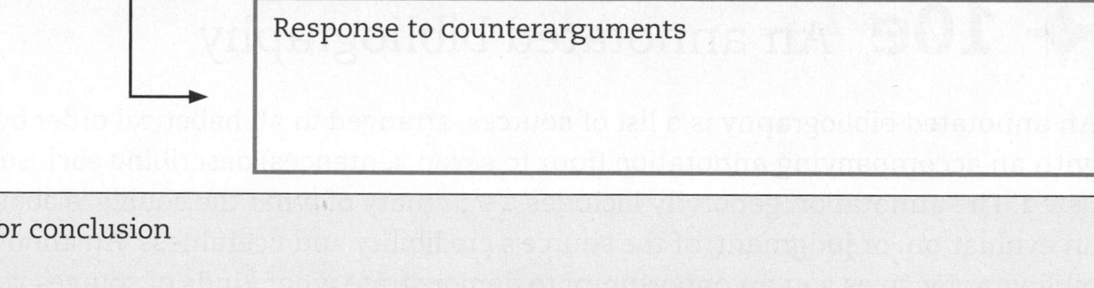


Ideas for conclusion

# 10e An annotated bibliography

An annotated bibliography is a list of sources, arranged in alphabetical order by author, with an accompanying annotation (four to seven sentences) describing each source listed. The annotation generally includes a summary of what the source is about and an evaluation, or judgment, of the source's credibility and usefulness. An annotated bibliography gives you an opportunity to demonstrate what kinds of sources you have gathered to help answer a research question and to reflect on what role each source might play in a larger project. An annotated bibliography has no thesis statement, no introduction, and no conclusion.

## Sample graphic organizer for an annotated bibliography

These boxes are meant to help you organize your thoughts. Your annotated bibliography may include more or fewer than four sources.

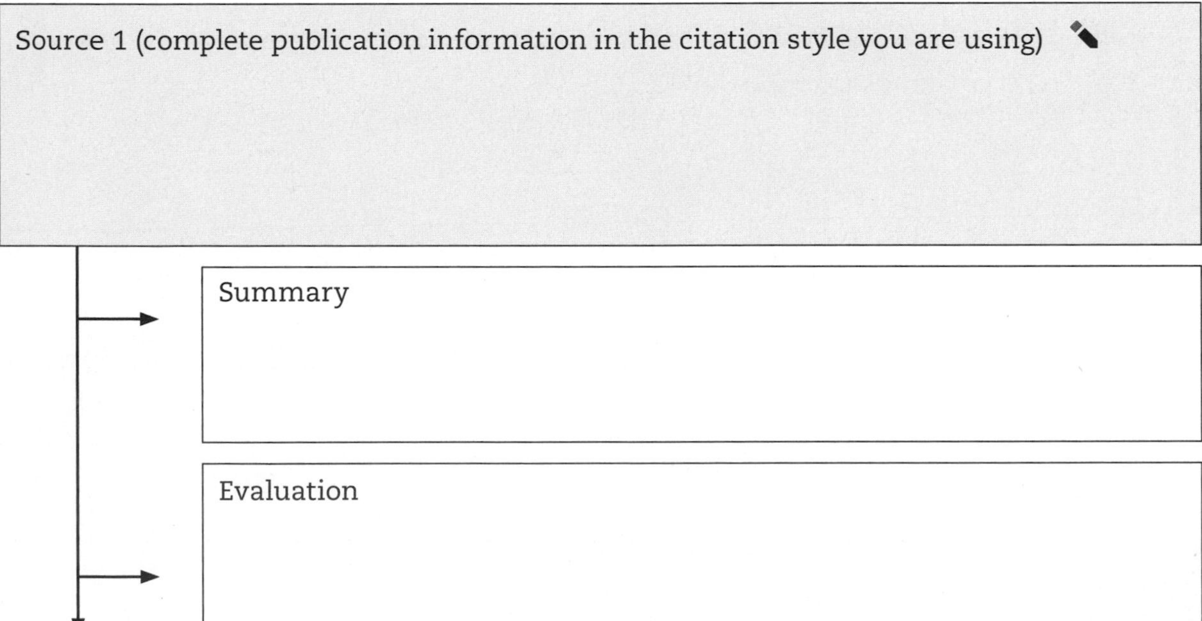

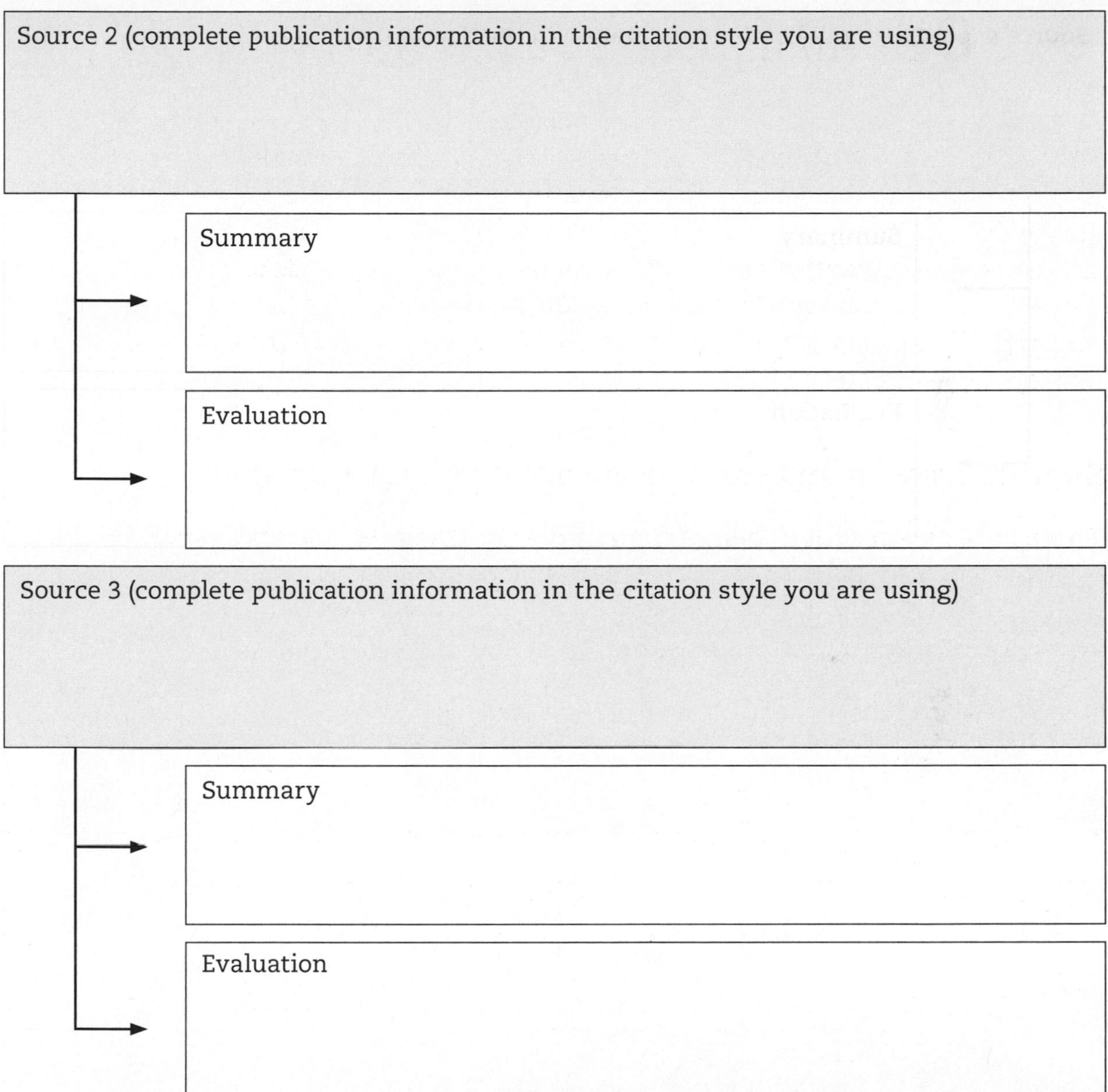
Source 2 (complete publication information in the citation style you are using)
Summary
Evaluation
Source 3 (complete publication information in the citation style you are using)
Summary
Evaluation

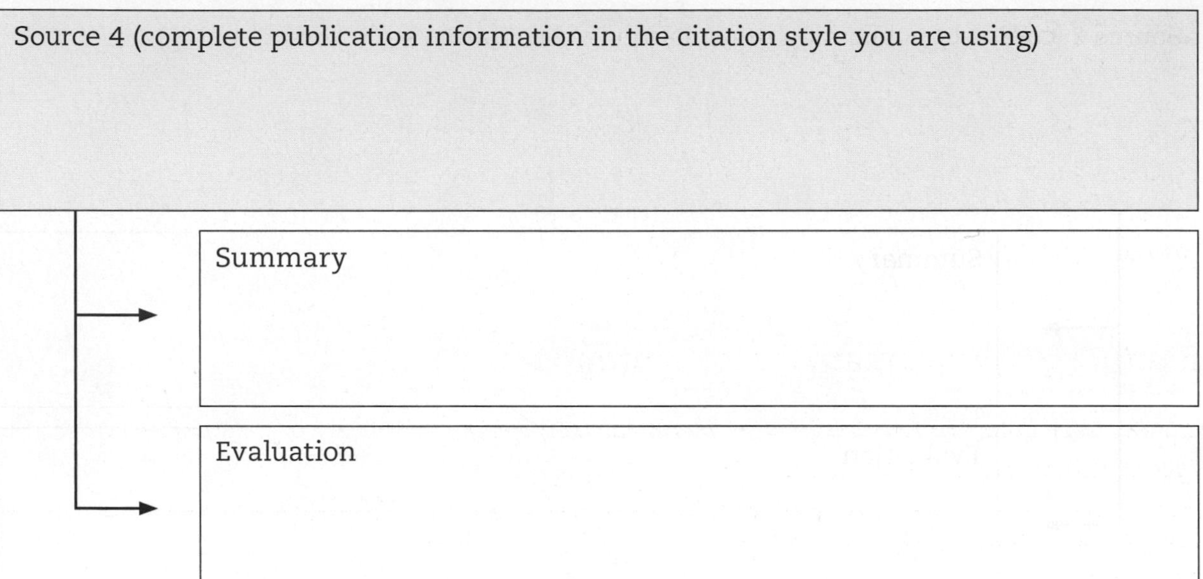
Source 4 (complete publication information in the citation style you are using)
Summary
Evaluation

# 10f A proposal

A proposal presents a plan and often makes an argument for something. In humanities courses such as composition, proposals are often associated with research projects or other projects. You may be asked to set forth a plan for investigating an idea, solving a problem, or answering a question.

## Sample graphic organizer for a proposal

These boxes are meant to help you organize your thoughts. They do not necessarily represent individual paragraphs.

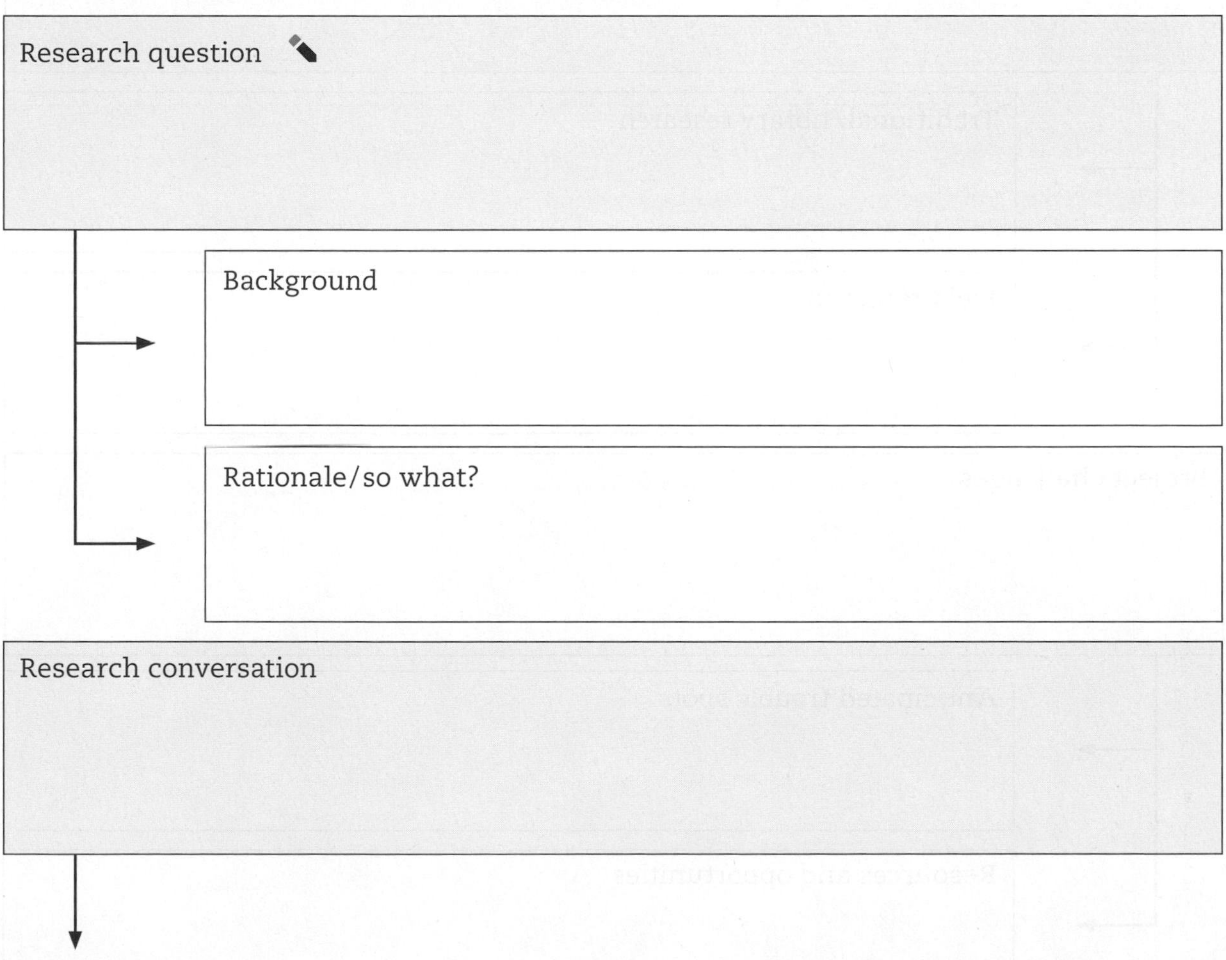

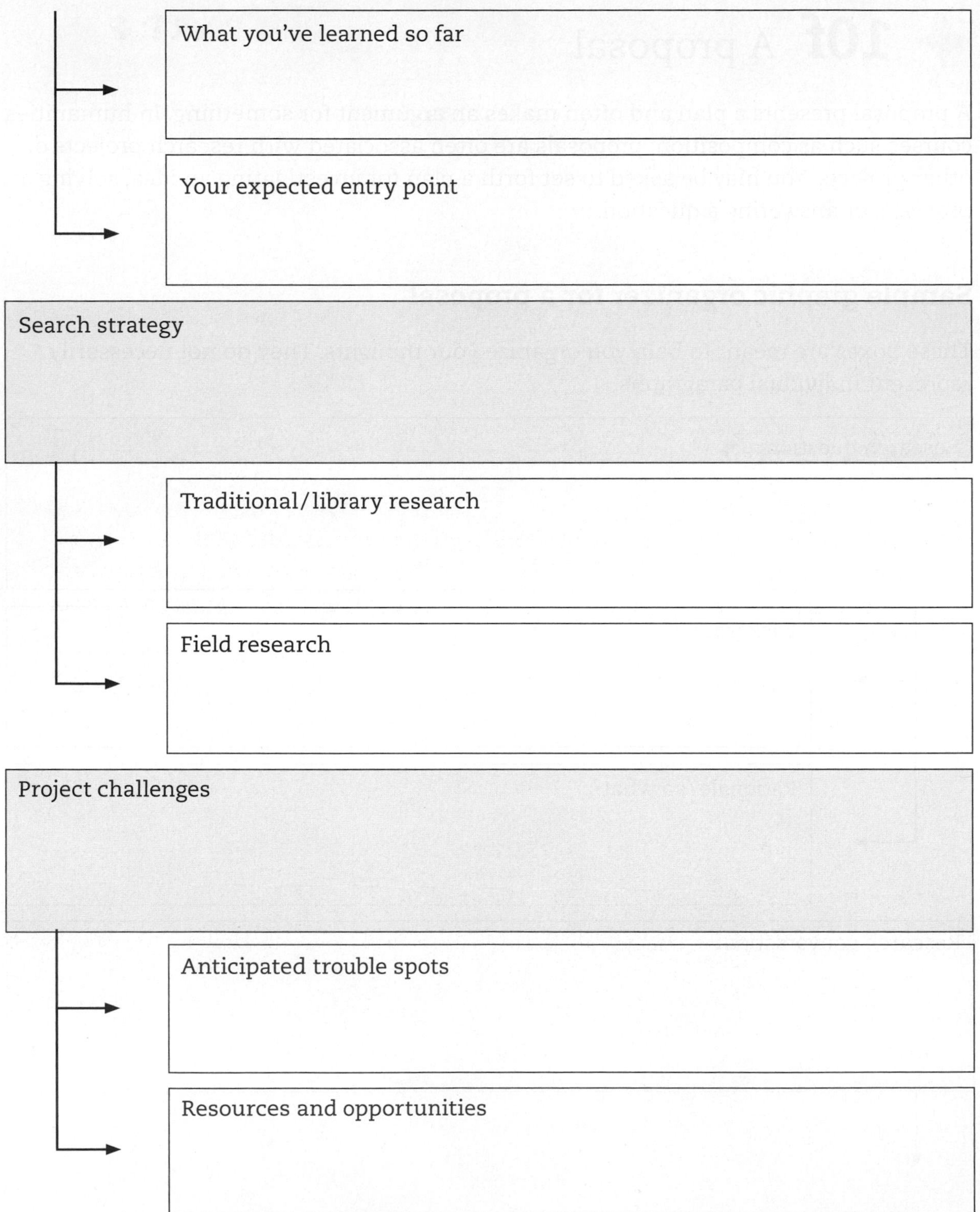
What you've learned so far
Your expected entry point
Search strategy
Traditional/library research
Field research
Project challenges
Anticipated trouble spots
Resources and opportunities

## CHAPTER 11

# Graphic organizers for common types of paragraphs

For students who benefit from a visual display of how certain ideas relate to other ideas, graphic organizers can be useful for drafting paragraphs as well as essays and other long works. The following pages offer graphic organizers for common types of paragraphs.

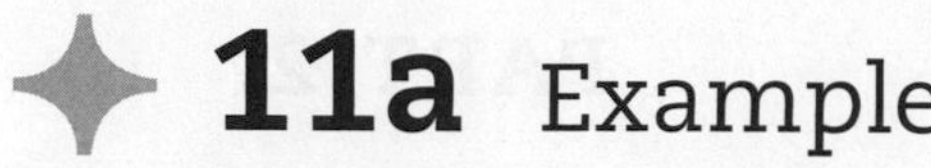

# 11a Example

Examples, perhaps the most common method of development, are appropriate whenever the reader might be tempted to ask, "For example?" A writer who starts with a general statement about how director Steven Soderbergh's films demonstrate substantial innovations in storytelling might follow up with a discussion of one or more specific examples of films with new kinds of storytelling.

This template can help you organize your thinking and your notes.

***General statement***

***Specific example***

***Specific example***

***Specific example***

## 11b Illustration

Illustrations are extended examples, frequently presented in story form. When well selected, they can be vivid and effective means of developing a point. A writer who begins with a general statement about how American Indian children get their names might develop the point with a detailed story of one particular instance of naming. The illustration would bring the general statement to life for readers.

This template can help you organize your thinking and your notes.

***General statement***

***Detailed story***

# 11c Narration

A paragraph of narration tells a story or part of a story in the service of a larger argument or other purpose. A writer might, for example, recall her experiences as a biracial child growing up in a predominantly black neighborhood to help her analyze the effects of race relations on children in America.

This template can help you organize your thinking and your notes.

| | |
|---|---|
| *Beginning of story* | |
| *Middle of story* | |
| *End of story* | |
| *Larger point* | |

## 11d Description

A descriptive paragraph sketches a portrait of a person, place, or thing using concrete and specific details and vivid language that appeals to one or more of the senses—sight, sound, smell, taste, and touch. A writer describing the aftermath of a devastating hurricane might use phrases such as *once proud and stately homes reduced to snapped and muddy twigs* or *the sopping upholstery smelled like ruin in the air*.

This template can help you organize your thinking and your notes.

| | |
|---|---|
| *Sensory detail* | |
| *+ Sensory detail* | |
| *+ Sensory detail* | |
| *= Concrete picture of a person, place, or thing* | |

# 11e Process

A process paragraph is structured in chronological order. A writer may choose this pattern either to describe how something is made or done or to explain to readers, step by step, how to do something. A writer communicating the process to follow in preparing for a job interview would begin with a statement about what the process is and why it is important or relevant to the audience. Using transition words such as *first*, *then*, *next*, and *finally*, the writer would detail the steps, in order, that the audience would follow to complete the task or understand how to do so.

This template can help you organize your thinking and your notes.

***Statement of the process and its relevance/importance***

*Step*

*Step*

*Step*

*Step*

## 11f Comparison and contrast

To compare two subjects is to draw attention to their similarities, although the word *compare* also has a broader meaning that includes a consideration of differences. To contrast is to focus only on differences. Whether a paragraph stresses similarities or differences, it may be patterned in one of two ways. One approach is to present the two subjects one at a time. A writer comparing the leadership styles of two modern heads of state might present all the qualities of one leader before moving on to all the qualities of the second leader. The other approach is to treat the two subjects together, focusing on one aspect at a time. For example, the writer might present the qualities one by one and compare the two leaders on each quality.

These templates can help you organize your thinking and your notes.

### First approach

***Statement about how two subjects are similar or different***

*Subject A*

*One quality*

*Another quality*

A third quality

Subject B

One quality

Another quality

A third quality

## Second approach

***Statement about how two subjects are similar or different***

*One quality*

*Subject A*

*Subject B*

*Another quality*

*Subject A*

*Subject B*

*A third quality*

*Subject A*

*Subject B*

## 11g Analogy

Analogies draw comparisons between items that appear to have little in common. Writers can use analogies to make something abstract or unfamiliar easier to grasp or to provoke fresh thoughts about a common subject. A writer making an argument about the benefits of after-school programs for low-income families might make a comparison between an after-school program and a life raft; another writer might draw a comparison between bumper-to-bumper traffic and a budget approval process for a social program.

This template can help you organize your thinking and your notes.

***General statement about X***

*Comparison of X to Y*

*Qualities of Y that are relevant to X*

*Larger point about X*

# 11h Cause and effect

A paragraph may move from cause to effects or from an effect to its causes. For example, a writer could point out the growing trend toward test-optional college admissions (the effect) and then discuss the factors (the causes) that have led many American colleges and universities to evaluate applicants without using SAT or ACT scores. Or the writer could show how new test-optional policies (the cause) have led to greater racial and economic diversity as well as a broader definition of talent (the effects).

These templates can help you organize your thinking and your notes.

## Effect to causes

*Effect*

*Cause*

*Cause*

*Cause*

## Cause to effects

*Cause*

*Effect*

*Effect*

*Effect*

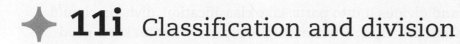

# 11i Classification and division

Classification is the grouping of items into categories according to some consistent principle. A writer may wish to classify students who take a gap year (the principle) into three different categories: students who want to earn money to make college more affordable, students who want to travel to build their independence, and students who want to volunteer to make a difference.

These templates can help you organize your thinking and your notes.

## Classification

***General statement to introduce the principle***

*Category 1*

*Category 2*

*Category 3*

Division takes one item and divides it into parts. Like classification, division should be based on some consistent principle. A writer might explore what makes a good cover letter for a job application (the principle) by dividing a typical cover letter into parts: the opening hook, the qualifications of the applicant, the call to action, and the professional close.

## Division

*General statement to introduce the whole*

*Part*

*Part*

*Part*

## 11j Definition

A definition puts a word or concept into a general class and then provides enough details to distinguish it from others in the same class. For example, a writer reporting on research about how companies determine whether their marketing efforts are effective might define *bounce rate* by first placing it in the class of business data and then offering details so that a reader would understand what the data defines or indicates and how it is used.

This template can help you organize your thinking and your notes.

*General class*

*Definition detail*

*Definition detail*

*Definition detail*

## 11k Reiteration

To reiterate a point means to repeat it or echo it. Some writers choose to do so for emphasis or intensity; other do so for clarity. In his 2004 speech at the Democratic National Convention, for example, Barack Obama made the point that America is defined by its overarching unity. He went on to echo the point in examples and language that reflected common ground and common bonds.

This template can help you organize your thinking and your notes.

***Main point***

*Echo*

*Echo*

*Echo*

PART 2

# CHAPTER 12

# Using sentence guides to develop academic writing skills

If you're a college student, then you're a writer, someone who makes sense of what you are learning through writing and who responds to a variety of writing assignments in any field of study. In most of these assignments, you'll be doing academic writing.

But just what do we mean by academic writing? The answer to this question can vary from field to field, but we can point to several features that almost all academic writing shares:

- Conventional grammar, spelling, punctuation, and mechanics
- Organization that links ideas explicitly
- Easy-to-read type size and font; conventional margins and spacing
- Explicitly stated claims supported by evidence
- Careful documentation of sources
- Use of conventional academic formats, such as research essays, lab reports, or literature reviews

Writing academically also means thinking academically—asking a lot of questions, exploring the ideas of others, and entering into scholarly debates and academic conversations. As a college writer, you will be asked to read different kinds of texts; understand and evaluate authors' ideas, arguments, and methods; and contribute your own ideas. In this way, you present yourself as a participant in an academic conversation. As an example, suppose you and your friends have an ongoing debate about the best film trilogy of all time. During your conversations with one another, you analyze the details of the films, introduce points you want your friends to consider, listen to their ideas, and perhaps cite what the critics have said about a particular trilogy. This is the same way conversations work in academic fields—except that scholars might be debating the best public policy for a social problem or the most promising new theory in treating a disease rather than film trilogies.

If you are uncertain about what academic writing sounds like or not sure you're any good at it, this chapter offers guidance for you at the sentence level. This chapter helps answer questions such as these:

> How can I present the ideas of others in a way that demonstrates my understanding of the debate?
>
> How can I agree with someone but add a new idea?
>
> How can I disagree with a scholar without seeming, well, rude?
>
> How can I make clear in my writing which ideas are mine and which ideas are someone else's?

The following sections offer sentence guides for you to adapt to your own writing situations. As in all writing that you do, you will have to think about your purpose (reason for writing) and your audience (readers) to decide which guides will be most appropriate for a particular piece of writing or for a certain part of your essay.

The guides are organized to help you present background information, the views and claims of others, and your own views and claims—all in the context of your purpose and audience.

# 12a Presenting information and others' views

When you write in academic situations, you may need to spend some time giving background information for or setting a context for your main idea or argument. This often requires you to present or summarize what is known or what has already been said in relation to the question you are asking in your writing.

## Presenting what is known or assumed

When you write, you will find that you sometimes need to present something that is known, such as a specific fact or statistic. The following structures are useful when you are providing background information.

**As we know from history, ___________.**

**X has shown that ___________.**

**Research by X and Y suggests that ___________.**

**According to X, ___________ percent of ___________ are/favor ___________.**

In other situations, you will need to present information that is assumed or that is conventional wisdom.

**People often believe that ___________.**

**Conventional wisdom leads us to believe ___________.**

**Many Americans share the idea that ___________.**

**___________ is a widely held belief.**

In order to challenge an assumption or a widely held belief, you have to acknowledge it first. Doing so lets your readers see that you are placing your ideas in an appropriate context.

**Although many people are led to believe ___________, there is significant benefit to considering the merits of ___________.**

**College students tend to believe that ___________ when, in fact, the opposite is much more likely the case.**

## Presenting others' views

As a writer, you build your own *ethos*, or credibility, by fairly and accurately representing the views of others. As an academic writer, you will be expected to demonstrate your understanding of a text by summarizing the views or arguments of its author(s). To do so, you may use language such as the following.

**X argues that ___________.**

**X emphasizes the need for ___________.**

**In this important article, X and Y claim ___________.**

**X endorses ___________ because ___________.**

**X and Y have recently criticized the idea that ___________.**

**___________, according to X, is the most critical cause of ___________.**

Although you will create your own variations of these sentences as you draft and revise, the guides can be useful tools for thinking through how best to present another writer's claim or finding clearly and concisely.

## Presenting direct quotations

When the exact words of a source are important for accuracy, authority, emphasis, or flavor, you will want to use a direct quotation. Ordinarily, you will present direct quotations with language of your own that suggests how you are using the source.

**X characterizes the problem this way: ". . ."**

**According to X, ___________ is defined as ". . ."**

**". . . ," explains X.**

**X argues strongly in favor of the policy, pointing out that ". . ."**

You will generally cite direct quotations according to the documentation style your readers expect. MLA style, often used in English and other humanities courses, calls for using the author's name paired with a page number, if there is one. APA style, used in most social sciences, requires including the year of publication, generally after the mention of the source, with page numbers after the quoted material. In *Chicago* style, used in history and some humanities courses, superscript numbers (like this[6]) refer readers to footnotes or endnotes. All three styles of in-text citations, like the ones shown on the next page, refer readers to entries in the works cited or reference list.

MLA Lazarín argues that our overreliance on testing in K-12 schools "does not put students first" (20).

APA Lazarín (2014) has argued that our overreliance on testing in K-12 schools "does not put students first" (p. 20).

*Chicago* Lazarín argues that our overreliance on testing in K-12 schools "does not put students first."[6]

Many writers use direct quotations to advance an argument of their own:

> **Standardized testing makes it easier for administrators to measure student performance, but it may not be the best way to measure it. Too much testing wears students out and communicates the idea that recall is the most important skill we want them to develop. Even education policy advisor Melissa Lazarín argues that our overreliance on testing in K-12 schools "does not put students first" (20).**

Student writer's idea

Source's idea

### Presenting alternative views

Most debates, whether they are scholarly or popular, are complex, as there are often more than two sides to an issue. Sometimes you will have to synthesize the views of multiple participants in the debate before you introduce your own ideas.

**On the one hand, X reports that ____________, but on the other hand, Y insists that ____________.**

**Even though X endorses the policy, Y refers to it as ". . ."**

**X, however, isn't convinced and instead argues ____________.**

**X and Y have supported the theory in the past, but new research by Z suggests that ____________.**

## 12b Presenting your own views

When you write for an academic audience, you have to demonstrate that you are familiar with the views of others who are asking the same kinds of questions as you are. Much of the academic writing that you will be assigned will require you to put your arguments in the context of existing arguments, in a way asking you to connect the known to the new.

When you are asked to write a summary or an informative text, your own views and arguments are generally not called for. However, much of the writing you will be assigned to do in college will call for you to take a persuasive stance and present a reasoned argument—at times in response to a single text, and at other times in response to multiple texts.

## Presenting your own views: Agreement and extension

Sometimes you agree with the author of a source.

**X's argument is convincing because ___________.**

**Because X's approach is ___________, it is the best way to ___________.**

**X makes an important point when she says ___________.**

Other times you find you agree with the author of a source, but you want to extend the point or go a bit deeper with your own investigation. You want to acknowledge the source for getting you so far in the conversation, but then move the conversation along with a related comment or finding.

**X's proposal for ___________ is indeed worth considering. Going one step further, ___________.**

**X makes the claim that ___________. By extension, isn't it also true, then, that ___________?**

**___________ has been adequately explained by X. Now, let's move beyond that idea and ask whether ___________.**

## Presenting your own views: Queries and skepticism

You may be intimidated when you're asked to talk back to a source, especially if the source is a well-known scholar or expert or even just a frequent voice in a particular debate. College-level writing requires you to be skeptical, however, and approach academic questions with the mind of an investigator. It is OK to doubt, to question, and to challenge because the end result is often new knowledge or new understanding of a subject.

Couldn't it also be argued that __________?

But is everyone willing to agree that this is the case?

While X insists that __________ is so, he is perhaps asking the wrong question to begin with.

The claims that X and Y have made, while intelligent and well-meaning, leave many unconvinced because they have failed to consider __________.

## Presenting your own views: Disagreement or correction

You may find that at times the only response you have to a text or to an author is complete disagreement.

X's claims about __________ are completely misguided.

X presents a long metaphor comparing __________ to __________; in the end, the comparison is unconvincing because __________.

It can be tempting to disregard a source completely if you detect a piece of information that strikes you as false or that you know to be untrue. But it's often a better idea to make clear how or why the information is false.

Although X reports that __________, recent studies indicate that this is not the case.

While X and Y insist that __________ is so, an examination of their figures shows that they have made an important miscalculation.

## Presenting and countering objections to your argument

Effective college writers know that their arguments are stronger when they anticipate objections that others might raise.

Some will object to this proposal on the grounds that __________.

Not everyone will embrace __________; they may argue instead that __________.

Countering, or responding to, opposing voices fairly and respectfully strengthens your writing and your *ethos*, or credibility.

> **X and Y might contend that this interpretation is faulty; however, ___________.**
>
> **Most ___________ believe that there is too much risk in this approach. But what they have failed to consider is __________.**

## A note about using *I*

Some disciplines look favorably on the use of the first-person *I* in academic writing. Others do not, instead recommending that you stick to using the third person. When you are given a writing assignment, either ask your instructor for guidance or look at sample texts you've received in class.

| **First person (I, *me*, *my*, *we*, *us*, *our*)** | **Third person (names and other nouns)** |
|---|---|
| I question Heddinger's methods and small sample size. | Heddinger's methods and small sample size are questionable. |
| Harnessing children's technology obsession in the classroom is, I believe, the key to improving learning. | Harnessing children's technology obsession in the classroom is the key to improving learning. |
| Lanza's interpretation focuses on circle imagery as symbolic of the family; my analysis leads me in a different direction entirely. | Lanza's interpretation focuses on circle imagery as symbolic of the family; other readers' analyses point in a different direction entirely. |
| We would, in fact, benefit from looser laws about farming on our personal property. | Many Americans would, in fact, benefit from looser laws about farming on personal property. |

You may think that not being able to use *I* in an essay in which you present your ideas about a topic is unfair or will lead to weaker statements. But you can make a strong argument even when you write in the third person. Third-person writing allows you to sound more assertive, credible, and academic.

## 12c Persuading by putting it all together

Readers of academic writing often want to know what's at stake in a particular debate or text. They want to know why they should care and why they should keep reading. In addition to crafting individual sentences, you must keep the bigger picture in mind as you attempt to persuade, inform, evaluate, or review.

### Presenting stakeholders

When you write, you may be doing so as a member of a group affected by the research conversation you have entered. For example, you may be among the thousands of students in your state whose level of debt could change as a result of new laws about financing a college education. In this case, you are a stakeholder. In other words, you have a direct interest in the matter, as a person who could be affected by the outcome of the debate. On the other hand, you may be writing as an investigator of a topic that interests you but that you aren't directly connected with. You may be trying to persuade your audience on behalf of a group of interested stakeholders of which you yourself are not a member.

You can give your writing some teeth if you make clear who is affected by the issue and the decisions that have been or will be made about it. The groups of stakeholders are highlighted in the following sentences.

> **Viewers of Kurosawa's films may not agree with X that ___________.**
>
> **The research will come as a surprise to parents of children with Type 1 diabetes.**
>
> **X's claims have the power to offend potentially every low-wage earner in the state.**
>
> **Marathoners might want to reconsider their training regimen if stories such as those told by X and Y are validated by the medical community.**

### Presenting the "So what?"

For readers to be motivated to read your writing, they have to believe that you're addressing something that matters to them, something that matters very much to you, or something that should matter to us all. Good academic writing often hooks readers with a sense of urgency—a serious response to a reader's "So what?"

Having a frank discussion about __________ now will put us in a far better position to deal with __________ in the future. If we are unwilling or unable to do so, we risk __________.

Such a breakthrough will affect __________ in three significant ways.

It is easy to believe that the stakes aren't high enough to be alarming; in fact, __________ will be affected by __________.

Widespread disapproval of and censorship of such fiction/films/art will mean __________ for us in the future. Culture should represent __________.

New experimentation in __________ could allow scientists to investigate __________ in ways they couldn't have imagined __________ years ago.

## Presenting the players and positions in a debate

Some disciplines ask writers to compose a review of the literature as part of a larger project, or sometimes as a free-standing assignment. In a review of the literature, the writer sets forth a research question, summarizes the key sources that have addressed the question, puts the current research in the context of other voices in the research conversation, and identifies any gaps in the research.

Writing that presents a debate, its players, and their positions can often be lengthy. What follows, however, will give you the sense of the flow of ideas and turns in such a piece of writing.

> __________ affects more than 30% of children in America, and signs point to a worsening situation in years to come. Solutions to the problem have eluded even the sharpest policy minds and brightest researchers. In an important 2003 study, W found that __________, which pointed to more problems than solutions. [ . . . ] Research by X and Y made strides in our understanding of but still didn't offer specific strategies for children and families struggling to __________. [ . . . ] Z rejected both the methods and the findings of X and Y, arguing that __________, policymakers and health care experts were optimistic. [ . . . ] Too much discussion of __________, however, and too little discussion of __________ may lead us to solutions that are ultimately too expensive to sustain.

*Student writer states the problem.*

*Student writer summarizes the views of others on the topic.*

*Student writer presents her view in the context of current research.*

## Verbs matter

*Using a variety of verbs in your sentences can add strength and clarity as you present others' views and your own views.*

| | | |
|---|---|---|
| When you want to present a view neutrally | acknowledges<br>adds<br>admits<br>comments<br>contends<br>notes | observes<br>points out<br>reports<br>suggests<br>writes |
| | **X points out that the plan had unintended outcomes.** | |
| When you want to present a stronger view | argues<br>asserts<br>declares | emphasizes<br>insists |
| | **Y argues in favor of a ban on __________; but Z insists the plan is misguided.** | |
| When you want to show agreement | agrees<br>confirms<br>endorses | |
| | **An endorsement of X's position is smart for a number of reasons.** | |

*(continued)*

| | |
|---|---|
| When you want to show contrast or disagreement | compares<br>denies<br>disputes<br>refutes<br>rejects<br>**The town must come together and reject X's claims that ___________ is in the best interest of the citizens.** |
| When you want to anticipate an objection | admits<br>acknowledges<br>concedes<br>**Y admits that closer study of ___________, with a much larger sample size, is necessary for ___________.** |

## CHAPTER 13

# Integrating sources: Quotation sandwiching (MLA style)

College writing assignments often call for you to read or view sources such as articles, reports, fact sheets, or TED talks and then use those sources as evidence in your own writing. Some sources will provide background information, others will offer data and statistics, and still others will make arguments for or counterarguments to your position.

One challenge in writing with sources is figuring out how to blend your ideas and the ideas of others smoothly. Chapter 12 provides sentence guides, giving you a sentence-level method for developing this kind of academic skill. This chapter offers a method for developing paragraphs in which you balance your ideas and the ideas in a source to move your argument forward. This method, which involves sandwiching source material between sentences of your own, is intended to help you show your readers how the source information relates to your claim or argument. By creating a context for your source material rather than just dropping it in, you can prepare your readers, which is much better than catching them unaware.

## 13a Integrating a single source

The following grid shows how one writer began to assemble a paragraph in which he discusses, as part of a larger essay on changes in digital culture, how social media can make people feel more lonely. The shaded part of the grid is the "meat"—the source material that helps the writer to make his argument.

| | |
|---|---|
| **Claim**<br>Your topic sentence for this paragraph | **It is surprising that with so many more ways to connect with others, more Americans than ever report feeling lonely.** |
| **Meaningful half-sentence (signal phrase) to introduce quotation**<br>Author's name, title, summary of the evidence | **In an article called "The Cure for Disconnection," journalist Jennifer Latson lays part of the blame on our digital culture and** |
| **Argument verb**<br>*suggests* *contends* *argues*<br>*affirms* *demonstrates* *insists*<br>*reveals* *emphasizes* | **argues** |
| **Quotation/evidence**<br>Direct quotation from text, using ellipsis (...) or brackets [to change words or word endings] as needed | **that "[c]onversations by text or Facebook messenger may be filled with smile emojis, but they leave us feeling empty because they lack depth"** |

| | |
|---|---|
| **Citation and period**<br>(Author's last name and page number) OR ("Abbreviated Title" and page number). If you mentioned the author or title earlier, you don't need it in the parentheses. If the source is a web source without pages, you don't need a page number. | **(49).** |
| **Explanation or paraphrase**<br>*Basically, X is saying that . . .*<br>*In other words, X argues that . . .*<br>*X suggests that . . .*<br>*X's point is that . . .*<br>*To put it another way, . . .* | **To put it another way, Latson suggests that we don't seem to feel satisfied by the interactions we have on social media platforms; this way of talking with others still ends up feeling impersonal.** |
| **Interpretation, significance**<br>*This demonstrates that . . .*<br>*This idea is important because . . .*<br>*Ultimately, what is at stake here is . . .*<br>*Although X may seem of concern to only a small group of people, it should in fact concern anyone who cares about . . .*<br>*And so, we should . . .* | **Although the problem of digitally induced loneliness might seem to affect mostly teens and young adults, more people of every age are having fewer face-to-face interactions, and the consequences could be significant.** |

Putting together such a grid can be a useful exercise; when you have your ideas and your source information laid out this way, assembling a paragraph can be much easier. See the following draft paragraph.

**SAMPLE COMPLETED PARAGRAPH WITH QUOTATION SANDWICH**

**It is surprising that with so many more ways to connect with others, more Americans than ever report feeling lonely. [*You may want to include more of your own writing after your topic sentence and before the quotation. That information goes here.*] In an article called "The Cure for Disconnection," journalist Jennifer Latson lays part of the blame on our digital culture and argues that "[c]onversations by text or Facebook messenger may be filled with smile emojis, but they leave us feeling empty because they lack depth" (49). To put it another way, Latson suggests that we don't seem to feel satisfied by the interactions we have on social media platforms; this way of talking with others still ends up feeling impersonal. Although the problem of digitally induced loneliness might seem to affect mostly teens and young adults, more people of every age are having fewer face-to-face interactions, and the consequences could be significant.**

Try making your own quotation sandwich by providing context before and interpretation after a source that you've chosen to use in your writing. Here's a blank grid. Keep in mind that the grid is intended to be a flexible guide. You may choose to make adaptations based on your sources and your purpose.

| | |
|---|---|
| **Claim**<br>Your topic sentence for this paragraph | |
| **Meaningful half-sentence (signal phrase) to introduce quotation**<br>Author's name, title, summary of the evidence | |
| **Argument verb**<br>*suggests* *contends* *argues*<br>*affirms* *demonstrates* *insists*<br>*reveals* *emphasizes* | |

| | |
|---|---|
| **Quotation/evidence**<br>Direct quotation from text, using ellipsis (. . .) or brackets [ ] as needed to alter the quotation responsibly | |
| **Citation and period**<br>(Author's last name and page number) OR ("Abbreviated Title" and page number). If you mentioned the author or title earlier, you don't need it in the parentheses. If the source is a web source without pages, you don't need a page number. | |
| **Explanation or paraphrase**<br>*Basically, X is saying that . . .*<br>*In other words, X argues that . . .*<br>*X suggests that . . .*<br>*X's point is that . . .*<br>*To put it another way, . . .* | |
| **Interpretation, significance**<br>*This demonstrates that . . .*<br>*This idea is important because . . .*<br>*Ultimately, what is at stake here is . . .*<br>*Although X may seem of concern to only a small group of people, it should in fact concern anyone who cares about . . .*<br>*And so, we should . . .* | |

## 13b Integrating more than one source (synthesizing)

You will often find yourself using more than one source to help you make a single point or to help you advance a part of your argument. This is what happens in most research writing, for it reflects the conversation that is happening about the topic. As the writer, you will be in that conversation, and you will weave in sources as you need them. In other words, you will synthesize multiple sources and show how the ideas in those sources relate to one another and to your ideas.

The following grid shows you one writer's notes for a paragraph in which he synthesizes multiple sources in the service of his own argument. Using the sandwich metaphor, you can consider this kind of paragraph a club sandwich with several layers. The shaded part of the grid is the meat—the source material that helps the writer to make his argument.

| | |
|---|---|
| Claim<br>Your topic sentence for this paragraph | **It is surprising that with so many more ways to connect with others, more Americans than ever report feeling lonely.** |
| Meaningful half-sentence (signal phrase) to introduce quotation<br>Author's name, title, summary of the evidence | **In an article called "The Cure for Disconnection," journalist Jennifer Latson lays part of the blame on our digital culture and** |
| Argument verb<br>*suggests* *contends* *argues*<br>*affirms* *demonstrates* *insists*<br>*reveals* *emphasizes* *maintains* | **argues** |

| | |
|---|---|
| **Quotation/evidence**<br>Direct quotation from text, using ellipsis (. . .) or brackets [ ] as needed to alter the quotation responsibly | **that "[c]onversations by text or Facebook messenger may be filled with smile emojis, but they leave us feeling empty because they lack depth"** |
| **Citation and period**<br>(Author's last name and page number) OR ("Abbreviated Title" and page number). If you mentioned the author or title earlier, you don't need it in the parentheses. If the source is a web source without pages, you don't need a page number. | **(49).** |
| **Transition to next evidence**<br>Signal phrase or half-sentence to link to a quotation from another piece that deepens, clarifies, builds on, or reverses the first evidence | **University of Chicago psychology professor John T. Cacioppo has found that people of all ages, however, deny their own feelings, but he** |
| **Argument verb**<br>*suggests* *contends* *argues*<br>*affirms* *demonstrates* *insists*<br>*reveals* *emphasizes* *maintains* | **contends** |
| **Quotation/evidence**<br>Direct quotation from text, using ellipsis (. . .) or brackets [ ] as needed to alter the quotation responsibly | **that "[d]enying you feel lonely makes no more sense than denying you feel hunger." He describes loneliness as an "aversive signal much like thirst, hunger, or pain"** |

| Citation and period | (qtd. in Hafner). |
| --- | --- |
| **Interpretation/significance**<br>*This demonstrates that . . .*<br>*This idea is important because . . .*<br>*Ultimately, what is at stake here is . . .*<br>*Although X may seem of concern to only a small group of people, it should in fact concern anyone who cares about . . .*<br>*And so, we should . . .* | **These ideas point to an important development in our psychological health. Our digital culture leads us to believe we have it all—and all a click away. But the emptiness that these researchers point to signals a need for something more personal and meaningful.** |
| **Short sentence or question for impact**<br>Short sentence to reaffirm your thesis, move your idea along, and break up the long paragraph—for example,<br>*But that's not enough.*<br>*We deserve more.*<br>*What can we do about it?*<br>*Where does this leave us?* | **So what can we do?** |
| **Transition to next evidence**<br>Third meaningful half-sentence to link to a quotation from another piece that deepens, clarifies, refines, or reverses the second evidence | **It may sound cliché, but Latner** |

| | |
|---|---|
| **Argument verb**<br>*suggests* *contends* *argues*<br>*affirms* *demonstrates* *insists*<br>*reveals* *emphasizes* *maintains* | **maintains** |
| **Quotation/evidence**<br>Direct quotation from text or a paraphrase or summary of the source's idea, which still needs a citation | **that the most basic thing we can do is to create situations that allow us to be our "authentic self with another person," which can mean practicing by getting together regularly with one or more people without our smartphones for an hour at a time** |
| **Citation and period** | **(50).** |
| **Reaction to evidence**<br>Analysis of the evidence—what this quotation demonstrates, reveals, or suggests<br>*X's suggestion is . . .*<br>*This quotation reveals . . .*<br>*This evidence demonstrates . . .* | **Latner's suggestion is a good one. Most people feel more satisfied after a substantial one-on-one conversation than they do after posting a fleeting thought and getting twenty "likes." We need the push-and-pull of ideas, eye contact, tone of voice, and other things that make us human.** |
| **Reaffirmation of link to thesis**<br>How all of this reinforces and advances your argument | **Although the problem of digitally induced loneliness might seem to affect mostly teens and young adults, more people of every age are having fewer face-to-face interactions, and the consequences could be significant.** |

The following assembled sample paragraph shows a balance of sources (highlighted) and original words of the student writer.

**SAMPLE COMPLETED PARAGRAPH IN "CLUB SANDWICH" STYLE (SYNTHESIS)**

It is surprising that with so many more ways to connect with others, more Americans than ever report feeling lonely. In an article called "The Cure for Disconnection," journalist Jennifer Latson lays part of the blame on our digital culture and argues that "[c]onversations by text or Facebook messenger may be filled with smile emojis, but they leave us feeling empty because they lack depth" (49). University of Chicago psychology professor John T. Cacioppo has found that people of all ages, however, deny their own feelings, but he contends that "[d]enying you feel lonely makes no more sense than denying you feel hunger." He describes loneliness as an "aversive signal much like thirst, hunger, or pain" (qtd. in Hafner). These ideas point to an important development in our psychological health. Our digital culture leads us to believe we have it all—and all a click away. But the emptiness that these researchers point to signals a need for something more personal and meaningful. So what can we do? It may sound cliché, but Latner maintains that the most basic thing we can do is to create situations that allow us to be our "authentic self with another person," which can mean practicing by getting together regularly with one or more people without our smartphones for an hour at a time (50). Latner's suggestion is a good one. Most people feel more satisfied after a substantial one-on-one conversation than they do after posting a fleeting thought and getting twenty "likes." We need the push-and-pull of ideas, eye contact, tone of voice, and other things that make us human. Although the problem of digitally induced loneliness might seem to affect mostly teens and young adults, more people of every age are having fewer face-to-face interactions, and the consequences could be significant.

You can use the following blank grid to assemble your own synthesis paragraph, making adjustments as needed for your sources and your purpose.

| | |
|---|---|
| **Claim**<br>Your topic sentence for this paragraph | |
| **Meaningful half-sentence (signal phrase) to introduce quotation**<br>Author's name, title, summary of the evidence | |
| **Argument verb**<br>*suggests* *contends* *argues*<br>*affirms* *demonstrates* *insists*<br>*reveals* *emphasizes* *maintains* | |
| **Quotation/evidence**<br>Direct quotation from text, using ellipsis (. . .) or brackets [ ] as needed to alter the quotation responsibly | |
| **Citation and period**<br>(Author's last name and page number) OR ("Abbreviated Title" and page number). If you mention the author or title earlier, you don't need it in the parentheses. If the source is a web source without pages, you don't need a page number. | |
| **Transition to next evidence**<br>Signal phrase or half-sentence to link to a quotation from another piece that deepens, clarifies, builds on, or reverses the first evidence | |

| | |
|---|---|
| **Argument verb**<br>*suggests* *contends* *argues*<br>*affirms* *demonstrates* *insists*<br>*reveals* *emphasizes* *maintains* | |
| **Quotation/evidence**<br>Direct quotation from text, using ellipsis (. . .) or brackets [ ] as needed to alter the quotation responsibly | |
| **Citation and period** | |
| **Interpretation, significance**<br>*This demonstrates that . . .*<br>*This idea is important because . . .*<br>*Ultimately, what is at stake here is . . .*<br>*Although X may seem of concern to only a small group of people, it should in fact concern anyone who cares about . . .*<br>*And so, we should . . .* | |
| **Short sentence or question for impact**<br>Short sentence to reaffirm your thesis, move your idea along, and break up the long paragraph—for example,<br>*But that's not enough.*<br>*We deserve more.*<br>*What can we do about it?*<br>*Where does this leave us?* | |

| | |
|---|---|
| **Transition to next evidence**<br>Third meaningful half-sentence to link to a quotation from another piece that deepens, clarifies, refines, or reverses the second evidence | |
| **Argument verb**<br>*suggests* *contends* *argues*<br>*affirms* *demonstrates* *insists*<br>*reveals* *emphasizes* *maintains* | |
| **Quotation/evidence**<br>Direct quotation from text or a paraphrase or summary of the source's idea, which still needs a citation | |
| **Citation and period** | |
| **Reaction to evidence**<br>Analysis of evidence—what this quotation demonstrates, reveals, or suggests<br>*X's suggestion is . . .*<br>*This quotation reveals . . .*<br>*This evidence demonstrates . . .* | |
| **Reaffirmation of link to thesis**<br>How all of this reinforces and advances your argument | |

# CHAPTER 14
# Revising paragraphs and essays

Revising is both difficult and rewarding, even for experienced writers. If you have never had luck revising, it's likely you just need more experience. Real revising—not just fixing mistakes—involves taking a genuine step back from a draft (putting it aside for a day or a few days) and then approaching the draft to answer key questions about your writing situation, overall purpose, audience, organization, evidence, and other global elements. Often, revising college writing involves seeking feedback from your instructor, peers, and perhaps a writing center tutor. Train yourself to focus on larger, more big-picture concerns in your reviews of your early drafts. You can make improvements in sentence structure, word choice, grammar, and punctuation later. It doesn't make any sense to puzzle over sentences that you may not keep from draft to draft.

For example, it might be tempting to fix some of the problems in this sample opening paragraph of an essay about the advantages of taking time off from social media. Before you spend time on spelling, capitalization, and punctuation, you might want to ask a few bigger questions:

- What is the main argument?
- Is it clear to the reader where an essay with this introduction is headed?

Being more social without social media

Social media is big part of american life especially the lives of 16 to 24 year olds. It helps bring people together and stay connected. But its not all positive. Stephanie Fairyington points out a "culture of comparison" that can destroy young people. Recent research points to growing numbers of cases of anixiety and depression. The real danger of social media adiction and mental health problems. Part of the problem is a digital identity disconnect where the you that you cultivate online doesn't match the you that you feel but you get tricked into seeing other's digital identity as reality. Another problem is that we are literally losing sleep waiting for likes to our posts. Giving up social media by taking tech breaks give us the chance to make gains socially that can't be made online.

In your own words, identify what you see as some of the bigger problems in this sample opening paragraph.

______________________________________________

______________________________________________

______________________________________________

______________________________________________

## 14a Tips for revising globally

The following tips for making big-picture revisions may come in handy as you revise your own writing.

**Re-read the assignment rubric or expectations.** Your instructor probably gave you a hard copy or posted a digital copy of the assignment sheet, which likely described the goals and expectations, length, due dates, and notes about the process for the assignment. Read the assignment sheet again before tackling your revision. If your teacher distributed a rubric or detailed list of grading criteria, have that handy as you revise. If one of the criteria is "A thesis statement that is debatable and sets forth your position," you will want to question, as part of your revision process, whether a reader could agree or disagree with your thesis.

**Approach global revision in cycles.** Global revision can be complex and time-consuming, so it's best to approach it in multiple passes or cycles. Leave yourself a whole day or evening to revise—know that you can't revise anything in a half hour. Make separate passes through your draft for each of these goals:

- **Clarify the purpose.** Look again at the expectations. Have you produced a draft that responds to the assignment? For example, if you set out to take a position but wrote a draft in which you largely present information and facts, or if you were expected to use evidence from sources but depended on personal opinion, you have an opportunity to pay closer attention to your purpose.
- **Improve the organization.** Look for opportunities to add or sharpen topic sentences, move blocks of text, or break ideas into separate paragraphs. Check to see whether your writing is organized in a way that makes it easy for readers to follow.
- **Tune your stance and message.** Consider where you might add specific facts, details, and examples. Look for opportunities to emphasize major ideas. Be clearer about where you are coming from and what your role is relative to your subject. What do you want readers or viewers to understand or feel about what you're communicating?
- **Engage the audience.** Look for opportunities to motivate readers to read on, to adjust the tone, or to change your appeals. If you think they'll object to certain points or language, for example, anticipate that objection in your revision.

**Pay attention to genre, design, and delivery.** Check the assignment again to see if the genre was specified. Is an essay expected, or are you able to produce a letter, brochure, blog post, or annotated timeline? Also be sure the design of your document matches what your assignment requires. Have you included headings, white space, and visuals that your readers expect? Finally, consider the final delivery: Is print or digital best?

**Seek feedback from reviewers, tutors, or other readers.** Many of us resist global revisions because we find it difficult to distance ourselves from a draft. We tend to review our work from our own perspective, not our audience's. Put your draft aside for a day or two, and then enlist the help of one or more reviewers such as classmates, family members, friends, or a writing center tutor. Remind them that you are focusing on bigger issues and will later turn to sentence-level mistakes.

**WRITING ACTIVITY ✦** What revision goals would you suggest to the writer of the following brief essay? Remember to focus on big-picture issues.

When people find out I play on a Special Olympics basketball team, they usually look at me sort of confused. I just smile.

As a lifelong athlete, I felt like I could really make a contribution when I joined a unified team two years ago. Unified sports teams place athletes with intellectual disabilities with athletes who don't have disabilities, and they compete together. I looked forward to teaching the game and the rules and mentoring some of the players.

Unified basketball games are exciting. I can see how someone would think it might be frustrating when a teammate takes off in a full sprint to score a basket for the opponent. But to see the pure joy on an athlete's face when they score—on any basket—is really indescribable. On a traditional competitive team, the competition can take over and change players; it sometimes makes them greedy and self-centered. On a unified team, the magic is in the name. It's a unified effort built around a love of competition and sport, but it's really more about support and sportsmanship. I went into my experience feeling like a little bit of an an expert, but I feel I learned much more than I taught.

Unified sports exist in some communities but not all. Many communities in the U.S. are searching for ways to teach young people tolerance and open mindedness, and starting unified teams through the Special Olympics organization could be one meaningful way to do that.

Problems with the draft (write them here or mark up the draft)

Suggestions you would make

## 14b Tips for revising sentences

When you revise sentences, you focus on strength and effectiveness. When you edit, you check for correctness, accuracy, and economy. Both are necessary—but after the main ideas, evidence, and organization are in place. Sentence revision, like global revision, may be approached in multiple passes through a draft. The main purposes for revising sentences are to strengthen, clarify, vary, and correct them.

Experienced writers have preferences for how to make revisions and corrections. Some writers do so directly in their digital document; others print a hard copy, make changes, and then go back to the document. If you are not confident in your proofreading skills, ask an instructor, friend, or tutor to point out some patterns or problem areas.

- **Strengthen sentences.** Look for opportunities to use more active verbs, to remove unnecessary words, and to choose language more appropriate for your discipline, subject, and audience. (Check your handbook for style, active verbs, wordy sentences, and appropriate language.)
- **Clarify sentences.** Think about where you can balance parallel ideas, untangle awkward or mixed constructions, replace vague pronouns, or define terminology. (Check your handbook for parallelism, mixed constructions, and pronoun reference.)

- ✧ **Vary sentences.** Look for opportunities to combine choppy sentences, break up long sentences, and choose different sentence patterns to vary sentence openings. (Check your handbook for variety, emphasis, coordination, and subordination.)
- ✧ **Correct sentences and verify accuracy.** Pay attention to the verbs you use, the sentence boundaries you create, and the punctuation you use. Also double check that any facts and statistics you have used are accurate. (Check your handbook for subject-verb agreement, fragments, run-ons, commas, apostrophes, and evaluating sources.)

Pay attention to the comments you receive on your drafts for the first several weeks of class. If you find you are getting similar comments draft after draft, a pattern may emerge and you can focus your changes. Keeping an editing log may help. In an editing log, you record frequent mistakes and note the place(s) in your handbook where you can find help. Knowing your patterns can inform your writing and revising processes on future assignments—whether in the classroom, in a job or internship, or in your everyday life.

**WRITING ACTIVITY** ✦ What sentence-level revisions would you suggest to the following paragraph in an essay that analyzes the song "Pumped Up Kicks" by Foster the People? You can edit directly below.

**The lyrics tells us about a boy, a "kid" whose "Daddy works a long day." He spends his day unsupervised Robert is alone in his house and all by himself and his free time is spent digging in "his dad's closet" trying to find cigarettes. There's not really a hint of any kind of relationship. At least a positive relationship. The father comes "home late" and Robert is left waiting "for a long time." Even if we can't relate to Robert. Maybe we can understand his actions threatening gun violence in his school could possibly be the result of an unloving home. Robert is a sympathetic character.**

# CHAPTER 15
# Reading exercises

## Exercise 15-a
## Using titles as on-ramps for reading

To read about this topic, see the section on on-ramps for active strategic reading in Chapter 6 of this workbook.

For each of the following titles, describe what you expect to read about and why. What can you tell about the author's purpose, audience, or approach from the title?

1. "Super Daddy Issues: Parental Figures, Masculinity, and Superhero Films"

______________________________________________

______________________________________________

______________________________________________

______________________________________________

2. “The Media Impact of Animal Disease on US Meat Demand”

3. “Student Nonsuicidal Self-injury: A Protocol for School Counselors”

## Exercise 15-b

# Using patterns of organization as on-ramps for reading

To read about this topic, see the section on on-ramps for active strategic reading in Chapter 6 of this workbook.

For each of the following passages, select the pattern of organization from the choices given, and then explain what clues led you to make that selection. How does knowing the pattern help you figure out the logic of what you are reading?

1. Is this paragraph organized by narration (telling a story), illustration (general statement followed by examples), or process (showing how to do something)?

   **As they confronted this devastating crime wave, black officials exhibited a complicated and sometimes overlapping mix of impulses. Some displayed tremendous hostility toward perpetrators of crime, describing them as a "cancer" that had to be cut away from the rest of the black community. Others pushed for harsher penalties but acknowledged that these measures would not solve the crisis at hand. Some even expressed sympathy for the plight of criminal defendants, who they knew were disproportionately black. But that sympathy was rarely sufficient to overcome the claims of black crime victims, who often argued that a punitive approach was necessary to protect that African-American community—including many of its most impoverished members—from the ravages of crime.**

   *Source:* Forman, James Jr. *Locking Up Our Own: Crime and Punishment in Black America.* Farrar, Straus and Giroux, 2017, pp. 10–11.

2. Is this paragraph organized by definition (telling the meaning of a word or concept), cause and effect (explaining the results of or reason for an event), or comparison and contrast (showing how two things are similar and different)?

**Let us begin with the critical differences between the missions and philosophies of the two federal agencies involved in regulating dietary supplements, the Food and Drug Administration (FDA) and the Federal Trade Commission (FTC). The FDA's mandate is to promote *safety*: its job is to ensure that conventional foods, dietary supplements, and drugs are safe and labeled accurately, and that drugs do something useful according to science-based standards—in other words, as verified by clinical trials. The FTC has a decidedly different mission: to promote *business competition*. One way it does so is by preventing unfair commercial practices such as false advertising. Thus both agencies are involved in regulating certain actions of supplement companies.**

*Source:* Nestle, Marion. *Food Politics: How the Food Industry Influences Nutrition and Health.* University of California Press, 2013, p. 227.

## Exercise 15-c

# Using vocabulary as an on-ramp for reading

To read about this topic, see the section on on-ramps for active strategic reading in Chapter 6 of this workbook.

As you read the following passage, circle any words you do not know, and then look them up. Pay particular attention to the word *modicum*. What does it mean? How do you know?

> **Square Foot Gardening methods save precious resources and help in the fight against climate change. These are low-cost, low-effort, space-saving methods of gardening that can be instituted just about anywhere, with a bare modicum of resources. Because of its rapid expansion and extensive humanitarian programs, Square Foot Gardening Foundation now reaches out to . . . sources of additional funding to help sustain its global and local initiatives.**
>
> *Source:* Bartholomew, Mel. *All New Square Foot Gardening: The Revolutionary Way to Grow More in Less Space*, 2nd ed., Cool Springs Press, 2013, p. 29.

## Exercise 15-d
# Examining a reader's annotations

To read about this topic, see the section on on-ramps for active strategic reading in Chapter 6 of this workbook.

In a pair or group, study the following excerpt from a scholarly article describing a study of distracted driving. Read both the article and the student reader's annotations in the margin, then discuss the on-ramps used by the reader.

**Excerpt from "Texting at the Light and Other Forms of Device Distraction behind the Wheel"**

**Cell phones are a well-known source of distraction for drivers (Redelmeier and Tibshirani). According to Strayer et al., the impairments associated with using a cell phone behind the wheel are on par with those of drunk driving ("Comparison"), and the US National Safety Council has implicated device usage in 26% of all vehicular crashes. The proliferation of text messaging services, web browsers and interactive apps makes modern devices even more distracting than voice-only cell phones. One may expect that as new features are added in years to come, devices will provide an even greater temptation for drivers to divert their attention from the primary task of operating their vehicles safely (Rowden and Watson).**

*main idea*

*on par = equal*

*compares distracted driving with drunk driving*

*rapid excessive increase (a negative word)*

**It should be intuitively apparent that manual interaction with a device while driving a moving vehicle will be dangerous. This claim is supported by studies that found that text-messaging was associated with more driving errors (Drews et al. and Mouloua et al.) and crashes (Issar et al.). Yet even with the vehicle at rest, interacting with a device may impose risks: the driver may not be able to respond quickly enough to sudden changes in road conditions, such as an ambulance passing through. In addition, texting may produce a lingering distraction that persists even after the device is put down (Strayer et al. "Distraction"). This loss of so-called "situational awareness" is reflected in an anecdote shared by a colleague (Endsley). He reported checking a text message while sitting at the light. After looking up and noticing that the light had**

*easy to see, figure out*

*examples of distracted driving in this paragraph*

*specialized term*

*story*

turned green, he rushed to accelerate—and promptly rear-ended the car in front of him, which had been slower to take off. Without situational awareness, "the drivers' eyes may be on the roadway and their hands on the steering wheel, but they may not be attending to the information critical for safe driving," as Strayer put it ("Technology").

*context clue — awareness of situation and surroundings while driving*

Interacting with a device with the vehicle temporarily at rest may represent a distinct form of driver distraction. Nonetheless, to our knowledge, a direct comparison of the rate of device usage by drivers at rest with the rate of device usage by drivers in motion has not been reported.

*lots of examples but no study of drivers at rest vs. in motion*

Significant usage differences between drivers at rest and drivers in motion, in turn, might have important implications for possible interventions aimed at decreasing this activity: if nothing else, safety processes that automatically shut down devices when the vehicle begins moving will not address texting at the light.

*does device safety not work at light? reason for study*

The research question we therefore address in this study is as follows: What is the incidence of texting with the vehicle at rest as compared with texting while the vehicle is moving? (For brevity, we will designate manual interaction with a device as "texting," though checking email, web surfing and other related activities would be included in this category.)

*these activities define "manual interaction"*

To answer the research question, we measured the rate of device usage for a set of vehicles stopped at a busy intersection, and compared it with the rate of device usage in a second set of vehicles that were in motion on the same road at a point just beyond that intersection.

*key word, purpose of study*

*Source:* Bernstein, James J., and Joseph Bernstein. "Texting at the Light and Other Forms of Device Distraction behind the Wheel." *BMC Public Health*, vol. 15, 2015, doi:10.1186/s12889-015-2343-8.

How is your group's analysis of the passage an example of active strategic reading?

______________________________________________

______________________________________________

______________________________________________

______________________________________________

______________________________________________

______________________________________________

## Exercise 15-e
# Using on-ramps to annotate and understand a reading

To read about this topic, see the section on on-ramps for active strategic reading in Chapter 6 of this workbook.

Use active strategic reading on-ramps to mark up the following reading and build an understanding of the article's meaning and message.

"Melting Ice Could Cause More California Droughts"

Loss of ice cover in the Arctic could spur more droughts in California, according to a new study by federal researchers. The study, published today in *Nature Communications*, finds that sea-ice loss in the Arctic could trigger atmospheric effects that drive precipitation away from California. The research was led by atmospheric scientists at the Lawrence Livermore National Laboratory.

It's the same kind of effect that contributed to [the] state's historic dry period that ended last year. The five-year drought was exacerbated by an atmospheric pressure system in the North Pacific Ocean that researchers dubbed the "ridiculously resilient ridge," which pushed storms farther north and deprived the Southwest of precipitation.

"[S]ea-ice loss of the magnitude expected in the next decades could substantially impact California's precipitation, thus highlighting another mechanism by which human-caused climate change could exacerbate future California droughts," the study says.

The study stops short of attributing California's latest drought to changes in Arctic sea ice, partly because there are other phenomena that play a role, like warm sea surface temperatures and changes to the Pacific Decadal Oscillation, an atmospheric climate pattern that typically shifts every 20 to 30 years.

The recent drought is also outside the study's scope because the researchers focused on potentially larger losses in sea ice than have occurred to date. The authors predict that over the next 20 years, California could see a 10 to 15 percent decrease in rainfall on average.

"The recent California drought appears to be a good illustration of what the sea-ice drive precipitation could look like," lead researcher Ivana Cvijanovic said in a release. "While more research should be done, we should be aware that an increasing number of studies, including this one, suggest that the loss of Arctic sea ice cover is not only a problem for remote Arctic communities, but could affect millions of people worldwide."

Conversely, sea-ice loss in the Antarctic would be expected to increase California's precipitation, according to the study's modeling. The North Pacific atmospheric ridge would be replaced by a trough, encouraging tropical storms to develop over the state.

Previous studies have hypothesized that the North Pacific atmospheric ridge is caused by increased ocean surface temperatures and movement of heat in the tropical Pacific. The new study elaborates on that understanding by describing the link between Arctic sea-ice loss and tropical convection.

The study could help narrow the range of uncertainty around how climate change is expected to alter California's precipitation patterns. Better modeling of Arctic sea-ice changes could improve prediction of changes in rainfall, the researchers said.

*Source:* Kahn, Debra. "Melting Ice Could Cause More California Droughts." *Climate Wire*, 5 Dec. 2017, E&E News, www.eenews.net/stories /1060068087.

## Exercise 15-f
# Talking back to a reading

To read about this topic and see an example of the strategy, see section 6g in this workbook.

For the reading on pages 154–155, "Melting Ice Could Cause More California Droughts," create a double-entry notebook page to identify specific passages and talk back to the author about the text, as a way to start an academic conversation.

| *Ideas/passages from the text* | *My responses/questions* |
|---|---|
| | |
| | |
| | |

# CHAPTER 16

# Thesis statement exercises

## Exercise 16-a
## Choosing effective thesis statements

An effective thesis statement is debatable, is usually an answer to a question or a solution to a problem, and uses specific language. From each of the following pairs, choose the better thesis statement for a first-year college essay. Explain your reasoning for each choice.

1. a. According to novelist John Steinbeck, why is it so important to have dreams and aspirations?

   b. John Steinbeck's novel *Of Mice and Men* teaches us, perhaps better than any other novel, how our dreams and aspirations sustain us in hard times.

_______________

_______________

_______________

_______________

2. a. An unused three-acre parcel of land behind the local high school has been evaluated for possible uses, including co-operative farming.

   b. It makes both economic and environmental sense to convert the unused three-acre parcel behind the local high school to a farm co-op.

______________________________________________

______________________________________________

______________________________________________

______________________________________________

3. a. In the wake of claims of racism by black and Latino artists, the music industry must act responsibly to reevaluate its guidelines for explicit content.

   b. The music industry's racist practices require explicit content advisory labels on music by black and Latino artists almost three times as often as on music by white artists.

______________________________________________

______________________________________________

______________________________________________

______________________________________________

4. a. The electoral college protects voters in rural and small states, and for this reason, the system must remain in place; moving to a popular vote system would create a sharp and undemocratic imbalance.

   b. The electoral college was designed for a number of practical reasons; one was to protect the interests of voters in rural states and small states.

______________________________________________

______________________________________________

______________________________________________

______________________________________________

5. a. Though it may seem drastic, classifying domestic violence as a hate crime, one that comes with far more serious penalties for perpetrators, is a useful step we should take to decrease domestic violence incidents.

   b. Decreasing the number of domestic violence incidents nationwide is an important goal, and new ideas about how to achieve it are critical.

_______________

_______________

_______________

_______________

6. a. In the film *Three Billboards Outside Ebbing, Missouri*, Mildred Hayes and Officer Dixon become unlikely allies—ultimately leaving viewers with hope even though the story's crime remains unsolved.

   b. In the film *Three Billboards Outside Ebbing, Missouri*, the relationship between Mildred Hayes and Officer Dixon is very interesting.

_______________

_______________

_______________

_______________

7. a. Lowering the drinking age from twenty-one to eighteen is a bad idea.

   b. Lowering the drinking age from twenty-one to eighteen is a workable idea only if paired with a drinker education program modeled on the classroom portion of a driver education program.

_______________

_______________

_______________

_______________

8. a. Because so many high school students cannot afford the tutoring that research has shown raises SAT and ACT scores, colleges and universities should remove these scores from their admissions evaluation criteria.

   b. It is unfortunate that so many high school students cannot afford the tutoring that research has shown raises SAT and ACT scores.

______________________________________________

______________________________________________

______________________________________________

______________________________________________

## Exercise 16-b

# Writing a thesis statement for an argument essay

The following brief argumentative essay includes no introductory paragraph and no thesis statement. Write a suitable thesis statement that includes the topic, a position, and some sense of the reasoning used in the argument. Once you've drafted a thesis statement, see if you can complete the checklist that follows the essay.

As an extra challenge, you might write an entire opening paragraph that includes a thesis statement.

**Telehealth is an exchange of data between patients and health care providers. A typical telehealth system involves two components, the first of which is a home monitoring unit. Patients use this technology to collect information such as their weight, temperature, heart rate, blood pressure, and oxygen level. The other component is a centralized monitoring station in a doctor's office or the office of a home health provider; this station collects the data and delivers it for a health care provider to review.**

**Telehealth monitoring allows elderly patients to receive health care without leaving home. The system allows them to communicate with a nurse remotely. Even though some might argue that it's healthier for elderly patients to be more mobile and to take more opportunities to leave their residence, a digital health**

**system allows patients the flexibility to receive care even when they choose to stay home—when the weather is bad, perhaps, or when they are not feeling well enough to travel.**

**Digital monitoring can also help elderly patients and their family caregivers to be more involved in managing the patient's condition. Being involved in daily checks of vital signs can give both patients and family members peace of mind. Often families of elderly patients report feeling helpless, especially if they are not able to attend occasional doctor visits with the patient. The telehealth system engages patients and family members and often facilitates a better understanding of the patient's condition.**

**Most importantly, a digital health system allows changes in treatment to happen sooner, which can often keep an elderly patient out of the hospital. The quick response is both a health benefit and an economic benefit for patients. When patients don't have to wait hours or days or longer to see a clinician, their chances of maintaining good health go up, and their out-of-pocket costs go down.**

*Thesis statement checklist*

_____ Does the thesis present a debatable point? *The thesis should not be a fact or description.*

_____ Does the thesis present an answer to a question? *The thesis should not be a question.*

_____ Is the thesis of appropriate scope for the assignment? *The thesis should not be too broad or too narrow.*

_____ Is the thesis sharply focused? *The thesis should not contain vague words like* interesting, good, bad, *or* wrong.

## Exercise 16-c
# Building strong thesis statements

For each of the following topics, develop a thesis statement that could work for an argument essay for a first-year writing course. You may find the checklist in Exercise 16-b helpful as you draft.

1. Concussions in college athletes

2. Student loan debt

3. Body cameras for police officers

4. Job interviews

5. Access to guns

6. Film trilogies

7. Learning to drive

8. Using mobile payment apps such as Venmo

# CHAPTER 17

# Topic sentence exercises

An effective topic sentence summarizes a paragraph's main point. Topic sentences help writers organize their ideas, but they also play two important roles for readers—they act as a preview for the ideas to come and as a kind of glue that helps readers understand the paragraph's point or its role in the whole essay.

Like a thesis statement, a topic sentence is more general than the material supporting it. Usually, such as in the paragraph below, a writer presents a topic sentence first in the paragraph and then follows the general topic sentence with more specific material that supports it.

> **In his "Letter from Birmingham Jail," civil rights leader Martin Luther King Jr. points out examples of civil disobedience throughout history. Early Christians in the Roman Empire, for instance, refused to renounce their faith and were persecuted. He also points to American colonists who threw tea overboard in defiance of the unjust laws of the British. Finally, he celebrates those who "aided and comforted" Jews during the Holocaust, a series of events that, at the time, were completely legal.**

Good writers preview their ideas with clues for readers, key words that announce what ideas will follow. The key words in the topic sentence above are "examples of civil disobedience" and "history." After reading just the topic sentence, you can guess that the paragraph is going to cover one or more instances of civil disobedience and one or more historical time periods.

## Exercise 17-a
# Choosing suitable topic sentences

1. Read the following paragraph, which does not include a topic sentence. Then, from the choices below, identify the statement that would be the most successful topic sentence for the paragraph:

   **First, increased perspiration could be a telltale sign of lying. Polygraph machines actually measure perspiration. A second giveaway relates to the touching of the face and nose. A person who is lying will experience an increased itching in the nose due to adrenaline. Finally, a quick and fleeting microexpression, such as the drawing upward of the eyebrows, could suggest that someone is not being truthful.**

   a. Physical signs can suggest whether or not a person is lying.

   b. Physical signs can suggest whether or not a person is telling the truth.

   c. Law enforcement uses advanced technology to detect lying.

   d. A psychologist can detect lying roughly 90 percent of the time.

   Why did you choose the answer you did?

2. Read the following paragraph, which does not include a topic sentence. Then, from the choices below, identify the statement that would be the most successful topic sentence for this paragraph.

   **One of the earliest superheroes in pop culture, Superman, first created in the 1930s, is sent as an infant to live on another planet. It's clear from early on that he doesn't blend in with his peers. Similarly, Black Widow is a Russian assassin forced to trade meaningful relationships for loyalty and duty to country. And Captain America awakens half a century in the future to an America completely unrecognizable to him. We love these characters for their "super" qualities but also for their vulnerabilities.**

   a. Superhero movies appeal to viewers of all ages.
   b. Because they are detached emotionally, superheroes are better at protecting ordinary citizens.
   c. Part of the emotional appeal of superhero characters stems from their depiction as outsiders and loners.
   d. Part of the emotional appeal of superhero characters stems from their deep patriotism.

   Why did you choose the answer you did?

   ______________________________________________

   ______________________________________________

   ______________________________________________

   ______________________________________________

   ______________________________________________

   ______________________________________________

## Exercise 17-b
# Writing topic sentences

1. The following paragraph is incomplete. Complete the paragraph by writing a suitable topic sentence.

   ________________________________________________________________________________________________________________________________________________________ **A 30-minute mid-day nap can be a stress reliever and can work just as well for college students as music or exercise. Even more importantly, naps can improve learning and academic performance (Weir, 48). Although some people feel that napping in the afternoon is a sign of laziness, it may actually be a sign that a student is more industrious and hardworking than his or her peers. The midday nap refreshes the brain for an extended period of focused study.**

2. The following paragraph is incomplete. Complete the paragraph by writing a suitable topic sentence.

   ________________________________________________________________________________________________________________________________________________________ **First, many Afghan girls are part of families that have been displaced by war and poverty, so access to schools is limited or just not a priority. Second, attitudes toward the education of girls in Afghanistan are still extremely conservative, despite the awareness raised in recent years by human rights groups and other education advocates. Finally, even when girls are enrolled in schools, they face the real possibility of physical and sexual violence as they make the trek from home to school, often with no transportation.**

## Exercise 17-c
# Writing unified paragraphs

Paragraphs are unified when they develop a single topic and when all of the ideas support the topic sentence. For each of the following topic sentences, develop a paragraph that demonstrates unity.

1. Musicians have always written songs about love. ________________

2. Sleep deprivation can have disastrous effects on college students' lives. ________________

3. There are important differences between having a job and having a career. ________

________________________________________

________________________________________

________________________________________

________________________________________

________________________________________

________________________________________

________________________________________

________________________________________

________________________________________

# CHAPTER 18

# MLA research exercises

## Exercise 18-a

## Avoiding plagiarism in MLA papers

For help with this exercise, see the section on avoiding plagiarism in MLA papers in your handbook.

Read the following passage and the information about its source. Then decide whether each student sample, numbered 1 to 5, is plagiarized or uses the source correctly. If the student's sample is plagiarized, write "plagiarized"; if the sample is acceptable, write "OK."

**ORIGINAL SOURCE**

**Smartphone games are built on a very different model [from traditional video games]. The iPhone's screen is roughly the size of a playing card; it responds not to the fast-twitch button combos of a controller but to more intuitive and intimate motions: poking, pinching, tapping, tickling. This has encouraged a very different kind of game: Tetris-like little puzzles, broken into discrete bits, designed to be played anywhere, in any context, without a manual, by any level of player. (Charles Pratt, a researcher in New York University's Game Center, refers to such games as "knitting games.") You could argue that these are pure games: perfectly designed minisystems**

**engineered to take us directly to the core of gaming pleasure without the distraction of narrative.**

*Source:* Anderson, Sam. "Just One More Game. . . ." *The New York Times Magazine*, 4 Apr. 2012, nyti.ms/1AZ2pys.

1. Smartphone screens have encouraged a new type of intimate game, broken into discrete bits, that can be played by anyone, anywhere. _______________

2. The smartphone touchscreen has changed the nature of video games: Instead of "fast-twitch button combos," touchscreens use "intuitive and intimate motions" such as "poking [and] pinching" (Anderson). _______________

3. As Sam Anderson explains, games on smartphones are "designed to be played anywhere, in any context, without a manual, by any level of player." _______________

4. Sam Anderson points out that, unlike older, narrative-based games that required a controller, games played on smartphone touchscreens can be learned quickly by anyone, regardless of skill level. _______________

5. Smartphone games can be called "perfectly designed minisystems" because they bring us right into the game "without the distraction of narrative." _______________

# Exercise 18-b
## Avoiding plagiarism in MLA papers

For help with this exercise, see the section on avoiding plagiarism in MLA papers in your handbook.

Read the following passage and the information about its source. Then decide whether each student sample, numbered 1 to 5, is plagiarized or uses the source correctly. If the student's sample is plagiarized, write "plagiarized"; if the sample is acceptable, write "OK."

**ORIGINAL SOURCE**

**We probably spend more time thinking and talking about other people than anything else. If another person makes us exuberantly happy, furiously angry, or deeply sad, we often can't stop thinking about him or her. We will often drop his or her name in our conversations with others, tossing in numerous pronouns as we refer to the person. Consequently, if the speaker is thinking and talking about a friend, expect high rates of third-person singular pronouns. If worried about communists, right-wing radio hosts, or bureaucrats, words such as *they* and *them* will be more frequent than average.**

**The word *I* is no different. If people are self-conscious, their attention flips to themselves briefly but at higher rates than people who are not self-conscious. For example, people use the word *I* more when completing a questionnaire in front of a mirror than if no mirror is present. If their attention is drawn to themselves because they are sick, feeling pain, or deeply depressed, they also use *I* more. In contrast, people who are immersed in a task tend to use I-words at very low levels.**

*Source:* Pennebaker, James W. *The Secret Life of Pronouns: What Our Words Say about Us*. Bloomsbury Press, 2011. [The source passage is from pages 291–92. Page 291 ends after *Consequently*, at the start of the fourth sentence.]

1. Adults spend more time thinking and talking about other people than they spend on anything else. ________________

2. High levels of emotion about someone may cause us to refer to that person more often and to use "numerous pronouns as we refer to the person" (Pennebaker 291).

   ________________

3. Pennebaker notes that people talking about friends will use "high rates of third-person singular pronouns" (292). ________________

4. Pennebaker explains that self-conscious people use *I* more often because "their attention flips to themselves at higher rates than people who are not self-conscious" (292). ________________

5. Pennebaker suggests that we can understand the way speakers regard those whom they are talking about by analyzing the pronouns the speakers use most frequently (291–92). ________________

## Exercise 18-c

# Recognizing common knowledge in MLA papers

For help with this exercise, see the section on recognizing common knowledge in MLA papers in your handbook.

Read each student passage and determine whether the student needs to cite the source of the information in an MLA paper. If the material does not need citation because it is common knowledge, write "common knowledge." If the material is not common knowledge and the student should cite the source, write "needs citation."

**EXAMPLE**

**The playwright August Wilson won two Pulitzer Prizes in drama.** *Common knowledge*

**[Winners of well-known prizes such as the Pulitzer Prize are common knowledge because the information is readily available in any number of sources.]**

1. Many of William Faulkner's novels are set in Yoknapatawpha County, a fictional part of Mississippi. ______________________

2. William Faulkner may have gotten the word *Yoknapatawpha* from a 1915 dictionary of the Choctaw language. ______________________

3. The writer and folklorist Zora Neale Hurston died in poverty in 1960. ______________________

4. William Shakespeare was the only playwright of his generation known to have a long-standing relationship with a single theater company. ______________________

5. Walt Disney fired and blacklisted all of his animators who went on strike in 1941. ______________________

6. William Wordsworth and Percy Bysshe Shelley were poets of the Romantic era. ______________________

7. As of 2012, the film *Titanic* had earned more than two billion dollars in box office revenue worldwide. ______________________

8. Heroic couplets are rhyming pairs of lines written in iambic pentameter. ______________________

9. Iris Murdoch wrote many sophisticated and complex novels before she succumbed to Alzheimer's disease. ______________________

10. George Lucas made a larger fortune by selling *Star Wars* toys than he made by selling tickets to *Star Wars*. ______________________

## Exercise 18-d
# Integrating sources in MLA papers

For help with this exercise, see the section on integrating sources in MLA papers in your handbook.

Read the following passage and the information about its source. Then decide whether each student sample, numbered 1 to 5, uses the source correctly. If the student has made an error in using the source, revise the sample to avoid the error. If the student has quoted correctly, write "OK."

**ORIGINAL SOURCE**

**More than 1% of California's electricity comes from the wind. During breezy early mornings in summer, the contribution goes even higher. "At those times, the wind accounts for up to 8% of our electrical load," said Mary A. Ilyin, a wind researcher for Pacific Gas & Electric, the country's largest utility and a major booster of wind power.**

**Half of California's turbines . . . are located in Altamont Pass and feed directly into PG&E's grid. Most of the rest are found in two other major wind centers: Tehachapi Pass on the edge of the Mojave Desert between Bakersfield and Barstow, with a capacity of 458 megawatts, and San Gorgonio Pass north of Palm Springs (231 megawatts). Both are hooked up to the power lines of Southern California Edison.**

*Source:* Golden, Frederic. "Electric Wind." *Los Angeles Times*, 24 Dec. 1990, p. B1.

1. Wind power accounts for more than 1% of California's electricity, reports Frederic Golden, and during breezy early mornings in summer, the contribution goes even higher (B1).

2. According to Frederic Golden, wind power accounts for more than 1% of California's electricity, and on breezy days "the contribution goes even higher" (B1).

3. Mary A. Ilyin reports that "wind energy accounts for as much as 8% of California's electricity" (qtd. in Golden B1).

4. On breezy summer mornings, says wind researcher Mary A. Ilyin, "the wind accounts for up to 8% of our [California's] electrical load" (qtd. in Golden B1).

5. California has pioneered the use of wind power. "Half of California's turbines . . . are located in Altamont Pass" (Golden B1).

# Exercise 18-e
# Integrating sources in MLA papers

For help with this exercise, see the section on integrating sources in MLA papers in your handbook.

Read the following passage and the information about its source. Then decide whether each student sample, numbered 1 to 5, uses the source correctly. If the student has made an error in using the source, revise the sample to avoid the error. If the student has quoted correctly, write "OK."

**ORIGINAL SOURCE**

**Most of us think that S.U.V.s are much safer than sports cars. If you asked the young parents of America whether they would rather strap their infant child in the back seat of the TrailBlazer [a Chevrolet S.U.V.] or the passenger seat of the Boxster [a Porsche sports car], they would choose the TrailBlazer. We feel that way because in the TrailBlazer our chances of surviving a collision with a hypothetical tractor-trailer in the other lane are greater than they are in the Porsche. What we forget, though, is that in the TrailBlazer you're also much more likely to hit the tractor-trailer because you can't get out of the way in time. In the parlance of the automobile world, the TrailBlazer is better at "passive safety." The Boxster is better when it comes to "active safety," which is every bit as important.**

*Source:* Gladwell, Malcolm. "Big and Bad." *The New Yorker*, 12 Jan. 2004, pp. 28–33. [The source passage is from page 31.]

1. Malcolm Gladwell points out that drivers feel safer in an S.U.V. than in a sports car because they think that the S.U.V. driver's "chances of surviving a collision with a hypothetical tractor-trailer in the other lane are greater" (31).

2. Gladwell argues that "active safety is every bit as important" as a vehicle's ability to withstand a collision (31).

______________________________________________

______________________________________________

______________________________________________

______________________________________________

3. A majority of drivers can, indeed, be wrong. "Most of us think that S.U.V.s are much safer than sports cars" (Gladwell 31).

______________________________________________

______________________________________________

______________________________________________

______________________________________________

4. According to Gladwell, American S.U.V.s are more likely to be involved in collisions than other vehicles "because [they] can't get out of the way in time" (31).

______________________________________________

______________________________________________

______________________________________________

______________________________________________

5. Gladwell explains that most people expect an S.U.V. "to survive a collision with a hypothetical tractor-trailer in the other lane" (31).

______________________________________________

______________________________________________

______________________________________________

______________________________________________

# Exercise 18-f
# MLA documentation: In-text citations

For help with this exercise, see the MLA in-text citations section in your handbook.

Circle the letter of the MLA in-text citation that is handled correctly.

**EXAMPLE**

**The student is quoting from pages 26–27 of the following source:**

**Follman, Mark. "Trigger Warnings." *Mother Jones*, Nov./Dec. 2015, pp. 22–29.**

ⓐ Mass shootings in America took a turn with Columbine; Follman argues that the teen shooters "authored a compelling new script at the dawn of the Internet age" (26–27).

b. Mass shootings in America took a turn with Columbine; Follman argues that the teen shooters "authored a compelling new script at the dawn of the Internet age" (pp. 26–27).

1. The student is quoting Christina Hoff Sommers from page 17 of the following book:

   Winegarner, Beth. *The Columbine Effect: How Five Teen Pastimes Got Caught in the Crossfire*. Lulu Press, 2013.

   a. In the wake of Columbine, according to Christina Hoff Sommers, "It has become fashionable to attribute pathology to millions of healthy male children" (qtd. in Winegarner 17).

   b. In the wake of Columbine, according to Christina Hoff Sommers, "It has become fashionable to attribute pathology to millions of healthy male children" (17).

2. The student is citing a blog post that appeared on the *Psychology Today* website:

   Ramsland, Katherine. "Mass Murder Motives." *Psychology Today*, 20 July, 2012, www.psychologytoday.com/us/blog/shadow-boxing/201207/mass-murder-motives.

   a. Katherine Ramsland describes motives for mass murder that "rang[e] from revenge to despair to free-floating rage at the world" ("Mass").

   b. Katherine Ramsland describes motives for mass murder that "rang[e] from revenge to despair to free-floating rage at the world."

3. The student is quoting from page 472 of a scholarly article by Dianne T. Gereluk, Kent Donlevy, and Merlin B. Thompson.

   a. Gereluk, Donlevy, and Thompson have called the teacher's threat assessment role "onerous" and have expressed concern about the "tremendous burden of watching for potential threats" in and out of the classroom (472).

   b. Gereluk et al. have called the teacher's threat assessment role "onerous" and have expressed concern about the "tremendous burden of watching for potential threats" in and out of the classroom (472).

4. The student is using statistics from the following article:

   Follman, Mark. "Trigger Warnings." *Mother Jones*, Nov./Dec. 2015, pp. 22–29.

   a. In the seventy-two known Columbine copycat cases, 53% of the planned attacks involved guns and 18% involved bombs or explosives (Follman 27).

   b. In the seventy-two known Columbine copycat cases, 53% of the planned attacks involved guns and 18% involved bombs or explosives.

5. The student is summarizing information gathered from a map found in this source:

   Mosendz, Polly. "Map: Every School Shooting in America since 2013." *Newsweek*, 16 Oct. 2015, www.newsweek.com/list-school-shootings-america-2013-380535.

   a. An analysis of the map reveals that there is no regional concentration in the occurrence of school shootings. They happen everywhere in America ("Map").

   b. An analysis of the map reveals that there is no regional concentration in the occurrence of school shootings. They happen everywhere in America (Mosendz).

6. The student is quoting the author's exact words from this online video:

   Gladwell, Malcolm. "Malcolm Gladwell Discusses School Shootings." *YouTube*, 5 Oct., 2015, www.youtube.com/watch?v=27aWHudLmgs.

   a. Gladwell's assessment of the recent history of school shootings is eye-opening: "It's an overwhelmingly American phenomenon," he says.

   b. Gladwell's assessment of the recent history of school shootings is eye-opening: It's an overwhelmingly American phenomenon, he says.

7. The student is summarizing the following unsigned source:

   "Another Day, Another Tragic School Shooting." *The Washington Post*, 9 Oct., 2015, www.washingtonpost.com/opinions/another-day-another-tragic-school-shooting/2015/10/09/62f5077c-6eb5-11e5-b31c-d80d62b53e28_story.html. Editorial.

   a. Mental health treatment and peer counseling are good first steps to reducing school violence; restricting access to guns, however, is the most important step (Editorial).

   b. Mental health treatment and peer counseling are good first steps to reducing school violence; restricting access to guns, however, is the most important step ("Another").

8. The student is quoting from page 45 of the following source:

   Klein, Jessie. *The Bully Society: School Shootings and the Crisis of Bullying in America's Schools*. New York UP, 2013.

   The list of works cited in the student's paper includes two works by Klein.

   a. Klein, a sociology professor, raises the idea that "boys are pressured to behave in a host of essentially superhuman or nonhuman ways" (*Bully* 45).

   b. Klein, a sociology professor, raises the idea that "boys are pressured to behave in a host of essentially superhuman or nonhuman ways" (45).

9. The student is paraphrasing from this short work from a website:

   "Effects of Bullying." *StopBullying.gov*, US Department of Health and Human Services, www.stopbullying.gov/at-risk/effects/. Accessed 5 Apr. 2016.

   a. Violence against others can be a response to being chronically bullied. There is evidence that many school shooters and mass shooters have experienced bullying (US Department of Health and Human Services).

   b. Violence against others can be a response to being chronically bullied. There is evidence that many school shooters and mass shooters have experienced bullying ("Effects").

10. The student is quoting from a blog post:

    Brucculieri, Julia, and Cole Delbyck. "These Classic TV Episodes about School Shootings Are More Relevant Than Ever." *Huffington Post*, 24 Jan. 2016, www.huffingtonpost.com/entry/school-shootings-on-tv_us_56a14986e4b076aadcc5c94b?utm_hp_ref=school-shooting.

    a. *Huffington Post* entertainment bloggers posted that a 2013 episode of *Glee* led some viewers to "[draw] connections between autism and Newtown, Connecticut, shooter Adam Lanza" and the show's Becky character (Brucculieri and Delbyck).

    b. *Huffington Post* entertainment bloggers posted that a 2013 episode of *Glee* led some viewers to "[draw] connections between autism and Newtown, Connecticut, shooter Adam Lanza" and the show's Becky character (Brucculieri).

## Exercise 18-g
# MLA documentation: Works cited

For help with this exercise, see the MLA works cited section in your handbook.

Circle the letter of the works cited entry that is handled correctly.

**EXAMPLE**

**The student has paraphrased information from the book *Breach of Faith: Hurricane Katrina and the Near Death of a Great American City*, by Jed Horne. The book was published in New York in 2008 by Random House.**

a. Horne, Jed. *Breach of Faith: Hurricane Katrina and the Near Death of a Great American City*. New York, Random House, 2008.

(b.) Horne, Jed. *Breach of Faith: Hurricane Katrina and the Near Death of a Great American City*. Random House, 2008.

1. The student has quoted from an article about Hurricane Sandy in the January 2013 issue of *Runner's World*. The article, "The Storm [and Everything After]," which appeared on pages 68–69, has no author listed.

   a. Anonymous. "The Storm [and Everything After]." *Runner's World*, Jan. 2013, pp. 68–69.

   b. "The Storm [and Everything After]." *Runner's World*, Jan. 2013, pp. 68–69.

2. The student has quoted from an article titled "The Katrina Conspiracies: The Problem of Trust in Rebuilding an American City," which was published in volume 35, issue 2, of *Journal of Urban History* in January 2009. The article appeared on pages 207–19 and was accessed using the *Academic OneFile* database at the URL go.galegroup.com.ezproxy.bpl.org/. The authors of the article are Arnold R. Hirsch and Lee A. Levert.

   a. Hirsch, Arnold R., and Lee A. Levert. "The Katrina Conspiracies: The Problem of Trust in Rebuilding an American City." *Journal of Urban History*, volume 35, number 2, 2009, pp. 207–19.

b. Hirsch, Arnold R., and Lee A. Levert. "The Katrina Conspiracies: The Problem of Trust in Rebuilding an American City." *Journal of Urban History*, vol. 35, no. 2, 2009, pp. 207–19. *Academic OneFile*, go.galegroup.com.ezproxy.bpl.org/.

3. The student has paraphrased information from an article titled "Hurricane Katrina as a Bureaucratic Nightmare," written by Vicki Bier. The article appeared on pages 243–54 of the anthology *On Risk and Disaster: Lessons from Hurricane Katrina*. The anthology was edited by Ronald J. Daniels, Donald F. Kettl, and Howard Kunreuther and was published in 2006 by the University of Pennsylvania Press.

   a. Bier, Vicki. "Hurricane Katrina as a Bureaucratic Nightmare." *On Risk and Disaster: Lessons from Hurricane Katrina*, edited by Ronald J. Daniels et al., U of Pennsylvania P, 2006, pp. 243–54.

   b. Daniels, Ronald J., et al., editors. *On Risk and Disaster: Lessons from Hurricane Katrina*. Vicki Bier, "Hurricane Katrina as a Bureaucratic Nightmare," U of Pennsylvania P, 2006, pp. 243–54.

4. The student has quoted information from a newspaper article that appeared in print on July 13, 2012, in *The Gardner News*. The article, written by Sam Bonacci and titled "Building Haiti Clinic Adds Up to Journey for Gardner Community," begins on page 1 and continues on page 4.

   a. Bonacci, Sam. "Building Haiti Clinic Adds Up to Journey for Gardner Community." *The Gardner News*, 13 July 2012, pp. 1, 4.

   b. Bonacci, Sam. "Building Haiti Clinic Adds Up to Journey for Gardner Community." *The Gardner News*, 13 July 2012, pp. 1+.

5. The student has paraphrased information from the article "How Weather Could Link Japan Radiation to US," which appeared on the *Scientific American* website (www.scientificamerican.com/article/weather-japan-radiation-united-states/) on March 16, 2011. The article was written by Jim Andrews and AccuWeather.

   a. Andrews, Jim, and AccuWeather. "How Weather Could Link Japan Radiation to US." *Scientific American*, 16 Mar. 2011, www.scientificamerican.com/article/weather-japan-radiation-united-states/.

   b. Andrews, Jim, and AccuWeather. "How Weather Could Link Japan Radiation to US." *Scientific American*, www.scientificamerican.com/article/weather-japan-radiation-united-states/.

6. The student has summarized information from a televised interview with Fareed Zakaria, conducted by Ali Velshi. Video from the interview, titled "Was Hurricane Sandy a Wake-Up Call?," was posted on the *Your Money* blog on the CNN website at the URL yourmoney.blogs.cnn.com/2012/11/23/was-hurricane-sandy-a-wake-up-call/?hpt=ym_bn2. The interview took place on November 21, 2012.

   a. Zakaria, Fareed. "Was Hurricane Sandy a Wake-Up Call?" Interview by Ali Velshi, *Your Money*, CNN, 21 Nov. 2012, yourmoney.blogs.cnn.com/2012/11/23/was-hurricane-sandy-a-wake-up-call/?hpt=ym_bn2.

   b. Velshi, Ali. "Was Hurricane Sandy a Wake-Up Call?" Interviewed Fareed Zakaria, *Your Money*, CNN, 21 Nov. 2012, yourmoney.blogs.cnn.com/2012/11/23/was-hurricane-sandy-a-wake-up-call/?hpt=ym_bn2.

7. The student has paraphrased information from a film on DVD titled *Japan's Killer Quake*, which was released by PBS in 2011. The film was narrated by Corey Johnson and directed by Rae Gilder and Tom Pearson.

   a. *Japan's Killer Quake*. Directed by Rae Gilder and Tom Pearson. Narr. Corey Johnson, PBS, 2011.

   b. *Japan's Killer Quake*. Directed by Rae Gilder and Tom Pearson, narrated by Corey Johnson, PBS, 2011.

8. The student has quoted from a document *Navigating the Unknown: A Practical Lifeline for Decision-Makers in the Dark*, written by Patrick Lagadec and translated by Peter Leonard. The document was published by Crisis Response Journal in Thatcham, United Kingdom, in 2013.

   a. Lagadec, Patrick. *Navigating the Unknown: A Practical Lifeline for Decision-Makers in the Dark*. Translated by Peter Leonard, Crisis Response Journal, 2013.

   b. Lagadec, Patrick, and translated by Peter Leonard. *Navigating the Unknown: A Practical Lifeline for Decision-Makers in the Dark*, Crisis Response Journal, 2013.

9. The student has paraphrased a blog entry titled "Katrina," written by Chris Matthew Sciabarra on his blog, *Notablog*. The entry was posted at the URL www.nyu.edu/projects/sciabarra/notablog/archives/000727.html on September 6, 2005, and the student accessed it on February 2, 2009.

a. Sciabarra, Chris Matthew. “Katrina.” *Notablog*, 6 Sept. 2005, www.nyu.edu/projects/sciabarra/notablog/archives/000727.html.

b. Sciabarra, Chris Matthew. “Katrina.” *Notablog*, 6 Sept. 2005, www.nyu.edu/projects/sciabarra/notablog/archives/000727.html. Accessed 2 Feb. 2009.

10. The student has summarized information from an article on the web titled “Post-Katrina Education Problems Linger.” The article appeared on the website *eSchool News* on August 30, 2007, at the URL http://www.eschoolnews.com/2007/08/30/post-katrina-education-problems-linger/. No author is given.

    a. “Post-Katrina Education Problems Linger.” *eSchool News*, 30 Aug. 2007.

    b. “Post-Katrina Education Problems Linger.” *eSchool News*, 30 Aug. 2007, www.eschoolnews.com/2007/08/30/post-katrina-education-problems-linger/.

## Exercise 18-h
# MLA documentation

For help with this exercise, see the sections on MLA documentation in your handbook.

Write "true" if the statement is true or "false" if it is false.

1. A parenthetical citation in the text of a paper must always include a URL if the source is from the web. ________________

2. The works cited list is organized alphabetically by authors' last names (or by title for a work with no author). ________________

3. When in-text citations are used throughout a paper, there is no need for a works cited list at the end of the paper. ________________

4. An in-text citation names the author (if there is an author) either in a signal phrase introducing the cited material or in parentheses after the cited material. ________________

5. When a work's author is unknown, the work is listed under "Anonymous" in the list of works cited. ________________

6. All authors are listed last name first, followed by first name, in the works cited list. ________________

7. When a work has no page number, it is possible that nothing will appear in parentheses to mark the end of a citation. ________________

8. In the parentheses marking the end of an in-text citation, the abbreviation "p." or "pp." is used before the page number or numbers. ________________

9. When a paper cites two or more works by the same author, the in-text citation includes at least the author's name and the title (or a short version of the title).
_______________

10. For a works cited entry for a web source, a permalink (static, permanent link) or DOI (digital object identifier) is preferable to a URL. _______________

# CHAPTER 19

# Plagiarism exercises

## Exercise 19-a

## Is this plagiarism?

Read the sections on avoiding plagiarism in your handbook. Also read the material on plagiarism (it could be called "integrity" or "academic honesty") on your school's website.

For each of the following scenarios, argue whether or not the student plagiarized.

1. Student A has just begun to work on a research essay. The length requirement for this essay is four to six pages. It is now the night before the essay is due, and the student has written only two pages. To fill in the rest, he goes to several different websites and copies and pastes paragraphs from them into the body of his essay. He does not change the words, and he does not put the paragraphs in quotation marks. He does, however, list a couple of the websites on his works cited page.

   Is Student A committing plagiarism? Why or why not? ____________________

   ________________________________________

   ________________________________________

   ________________________________________

   ________________________________________

   ________________________________________

2. Student B is having trouble with her research essay. She has one page written, and she has found great sources, but she is having difficulty with the organizational structure of the essay. She goes to the Writing Center on campus, where a tutor helps her organize her ideas and cite her sources correctly.

   Is Student B committing plagiarism? Why or why not? ____________________

   ____________________

   ____________________

   ____________________

   ____________________

   ____________________

3. Student C purchases an essay online. She pays the full price, and the site assures her that she now owns the essay. She puts her name on the top, prints the essay, and turns it in.

   Is Student C committing plagiarism? Why or why not? ____________________

   ____________________

   ____________________

   ____________________

   ____________________

   ____________________

4. While writing a research essay, Student D uses language directly from Wikipedia. He does not use quotation marks, but he does indicate that the language came from this website by stating in the essay, "According to Wikipedia, . . ."

   Is Student D committing plagiarism? Why or why not? ____________________

   ____________________

   ____________________

   ____________________

   ____________________

   ____________________

5. Student E is writing a research essay. He goes to a website and finds a lot of great information to use in his essay. He paraphrases (puts the material in his own words), but he does not cite the source of the information or include a works cited list.

   Is Student E committing plagiarism? Why or why not? ____________________

   ________________________________________

   ________________________________________

   ________________________________________

   ________________________________________

   ________________________________________

## Exercise 19-b
# Developing responsibility

Imagine that you are mentoring a small group of high school students. The students do not have a lot of experience with academic writing. Reflecting on your own experience, and perhaps referring to the advice in your handbook, write five tips for your students on how to become a responsible writer and avoid plagiarism.

1. ______________________________

2. ______________________________

3. ______________________________

4. ______________________________

5. ______________________________

PART 3

# CHAPTER 20
# Paraphrase and summary exercises

## Exercise 20-a
## Building understanding (writing a summary)

Read the following passage three or four times; also read the title of the book that the passage is taken from. Then complete steps 1 through 6.

> **Now just because I identify with my people doesn't mean that I don't understand and grapple with what it means to be white in America. In fact, I was trained in your schools and I now teach your children. But I remain what I was when I started my vocation, my pilgrimage of self-discovery: a black preacher. It is for that reason that I don't want to—really, I can't afford to—give up on the possibility that white America can definitively, finally, hear from one black American preacher a plea, a cry, a sermon, from my heart to yours.**
>
> *Source:* Dyson, Michael Eric. *Tears We Cannot Stop: A Sermon to White America*. St. Martin's Press, 2017, pp. 5–6.

1. What can you tell about this reading or its author, Michael Eric Dyson, just from the title of the book? ______________________________

______________________________

______________________________

2. Make notes on the passage. Write down, circle, highlight, or define anything you think might help you understand what this passage is about.

**Now just because I identify with my people doesn't mean that I don't understand and grapple with what it means to be white in America. In fact, I was trained in your schools and I now teach your children. But I remain what I was when I started my vocation, my pilgrimage of self-discovery: a black preacher. It is for that reason that I don't want to—really, I can't afford to—give up on the possibility that white America can definitively, finally, hear from one black American preacher a plea, a cry, a sermon, from my heart to yours.**

3. Read the passage and your notes one more time. Then, WITHOUT LOOKING at the passage, write down the author's basic message or main idea, as you understand it.

______________________________

______________________________

______________________________

______________________________

______________________________

4. Write a one-sentence summary that communicates your understanding of the author's main idea.

   ______________________________________________

   ______________________________________________

   ______________________________________________

   ______________________________________________

   ______________________________________________

5. If you have used any exact language from Dyson's passage, go back and put those words in quotation marks.

6. You still must cite a source even if you summarize it in your own words. Add a citation at the end of your summary sentence—either the author's last name and the page numbers in parentheses or, if you mentioned the author's last name in your sentence, just the page numbers in parentheses.

## Exercise 20-b

# Using your own words and structure (writing a paraphrase)

Read the following passage three or four times; also read the title of the book that the passage is taken from. Then complete steps 1 through 6.

> **Durable, robust learning requires that we do two things. First, as we recode and consolidate new material from short-term memory into long-term memory, we must anchor it there securely. Second, we must associate the material with a diverse set of cues that will make us adept at recalling the knowledge later. Having effective retrieval cues is an aspect of learning that often goes overlooked. The task is more than committing knowledge to memory. Being able to retrieve it when we need it is just as important.**
>
> *Source:* Brown, Peter C., Henry L. Roediger III, and Mark A. McDaniel. *Make It Stick: The Science of Successful Learning.* Harvard UP, 2014, p. 75.

1. What can you tell about this reading just from the title of the book? ______________

_______________________________________________

_______________________________________________

_______________________________________________

2. Make notes on the passage. Write down, circle, highlight, or define anything you think might help you understand what this passage is about.

   **Durable, robust learning requires that we do two things. First, as we recode and consolidate new material from short-term memory into long-term memory, we must anchor it there securely. Second, we must associate the material with a diverse set of cues that will make us adept at recalling the knowledge later. Having effective**

**retrieval cues is an aspect of learning that often goes overlooked. The task is more than committing knowledge to memory. Being able to retrieve it when we need it is just as important.**

3. Read the passage and your notes one more time. Then WITHOUT LOOKING at the passage, write down the authors' basic message or main idea, as you understand it.

4. Paraphrasing a source requires you to capture the ideas from the source in roughly the same amount of words and sentences. Paraphrasing responsibly means using your own words *and* using your own sentence structure. Your paraphrase shouldn't be organized in the same way as the original, and it shouldn't just substitute occasional words for the source's words. The original passage above is six sentences. Write a paraphrase of roughly five to seven sentences using your own language and organization.

5. If you have used any exact language from the authors, go back and put those words in quotation marks.

6. You still must cite a source even if you paraphrase it in your own words. Add a citation at the end of your summary sentence—either the first author's last name and the page number in parentheses or, if you mentioned the authors in your sentence, just the page number in parentheses. (Hint: For three or more authors, use *et al.* for "and others." Here's an example: Nuñez et al. 37.)

## Exercise 20-c
# Writing paraphrases and summaries

Read the following passage. From the options that follow the passage, choose the summary that is written more responsibly, and explain your reasoning.

> **Food companies use every means at their disposal . . . to create and protect an environment that is conducive to selling their products in a competitive marketplace. To begin with, they lobby. They lobby Congress for favorable laws, government agencies for favorable regulations, and the White House for favorable trade agreements. But lobbying is only the most obvious of their methods. Far less visible are the arrangements made with food and nutrition experts to obtain approving judgments about the nutritional quality or health benefits of food products.**
>
> *Source:* Nestle, Marion. *Food Politics: How the Food Industry Influences Nutrition and Health.* U of California P, 2013, p. 93.

1. a. Beyond the expected strategy, lobbying US legislators, food manufacturers also strategize to get experts in the field to say that their products are healthy and nutritious (Nestle 93).

   b. Beyond lobbying Congress for favorable laws, food manufacturers also strategize to obtain approving judgments about the nutritional quality of food from experts in the field (Nestle 93).

   Which is the more responsible summary? ______________________

   Explain your reasoning. ______________________

   ______________________

   ______________________

   ______________________

   ______________________

Review the passage on the previous page. Then, from the options below, choose the paraphrase that is written more responsibly, and explain your reasoning.

2. a. Policy expert Marion Nestle points out that high competition requires food manufacturers to use many different strategies. One strategy is that they lobby for trade agreements, rules, and laws that benefit their sales and marketing efforts. Another strategy, perhaps not so apparent, involves trying to get health experts to vouch for their products as healthy and beneficial (93).

   b. Policy expert Marion Nestle points out that food manufacturers use many different strategies to create the best environment for their success. One strategy is that they lobby. They lobby for trade agreements, rules, and laws that benefit their sales and marketing efforts. But lobbying is only the most apparent strategy. Another strategy, perhaps not so apparent, involves trying to get health experts to pass approving judgments of the products as healthy and beneficial (93).

Which is the more responsible paraphrase? ______________________

Explain your reasoning. ______________________

______________________

______________________

______________________

______________________

Bonus: Explain why the citations in item 2 above have just a page number in parentheses while the citations in item 1 have a name and a page number. Is one style right and the other wrong? ______________________

______________________

______________________

______________________

______________________

# CHAPTER 21

# Active verbs

## Exercise 21-a

## Active verbs (Editing sentences)

To read about this topic, see the section on active verbs in your handbook.

Underline each *be* verb and the past participle that follows it. Then rewrite the sentence so that the verbs are active. Example:

**A rake was carelessly left in the yard by the gardener.**

*The gardener carelessly left a rake in the yard.*

1. This computer was used by me.

2. In Japan, only major streets are provided with names by cities.

3. Television advertisements for wine are banned by France's government.

4. The tuition increase was announced by the college president.

5. A cameo appearance was made by Vice President Joe Biden in a fifth-season episode of *Parks and Recreation*.

## Exercise 21-b

# Active verbs (Editing sentences)

To read about this topic, see the section on active verbs in your handbook.

Some of the following sentences contain passive verbs or verbs that are a form of *be*. Find them and change them to active verbs. You may need to invent a subject for some verbs. If a sentence does not contain a passive verb, mark it as "active." Example:

> T passed the bill.
>
> ~~The bill was passed by~~ ~~t~~he Senate/ ^

1. Supper was prepared by Jim.

2. When she is ready, she will tee up and take a swing at the golf ball.

3. In 2013, Beyoncé was invited by President Obama to perform at the presidential inaugural gala.

4. Parker is too embarrassed to tell his manager that the deadline was missed.

5. Everyone was affected by the recession.

## Exercise 21-c
# Active verbs (Editing paragraphs)

To read about this topic, see the section on active verbs in your handbook.

In the following paragraph, revise any weak or unemphatic sentences by replacing any passive verbs, or *be* verbs, with active verbs. The first revision has been done for you.

*pop culture enthusiasts define cosplay*

In general, ~~cosplay is defined by pop culture enthusiasts~~ as an activity in which costumes based on characters from popular culture are worn by people. Movies, television shows, comic books, and even video games are where these characters come from. The term *cosplay* is a combination of two words: *costume* and *play*. While cosplay might seem like just another form of dressing up, it is considered a distinct cultural activity by fans, not the same thing as Halloween or a costume party.

Cosplay once appealed to only a tiny segment of the population. It was first practiced by enthusiastic fans of Japanese animation in the 1990s. Today, cosplay is done by thousands of people. Cosplayers aren't just serious anime fans anymore; all different kinds of characters are cosplayed, and events are attended in costume by all levels of fans, from the casual to the obsessed. Fan conventions are now a huge business. Events like Comic-Con in San Diego and New York, Dragon Con in Atlanta, and Anime Vegas in Las Vegas are attended widely by cosplayers and non-cosplayers alike. The rise in cosplayers is attributed by some pop culture enthusiasts to the popularity of other formerly "nerdy" things. Comic book movies and shows like the Marvel Cinematic Universe, fantasy series like *Game of Thrones* and *Harry Potter*, and sci-fi movies like the *Star Wars* series are loved by almost everyone.

# CHAPTER 22
# Parallelism

## Exercise 22-a
## Parallelism (Editing sentences)

To read about this topic, see the section on parallelism in your handbook.

Identify and correct errors in parallelism for each of the following sentences. Example:

> **I want to improve my computer skills by taking online classes, learning to code, and** studying blog posts by industry experts.
> ~~I'll study blog posts by industry experts.~~
> ^

1. Dr. Sanchez taught me to write more clearly, to avoid grammatical errors, and punctuality.
2. A good story requires both an introduction that grabs readers' attention and ends with a satisfying conclusion.
3. I would rather you ask for directions than getting lost.
4. Tiana had to feed the cat, water the plants, and the pet sitter needed a house key.
5. Hedy Lamar was not only an actress, but also was an inventor who helped to create the technology that led to Wi-Fi and Bluetooth.

## Exercise 22-b
# Parallelism (Editing sentences)

To read about this topic, see the section on parallelism in your handbook.

Circle the letter of the option that best completes the parallel structure of each sentence. Example:

**The children are eager to open their presents and ________.**

**a. playing with their new toys**

**(b.) play with their new toys**

**c. their new toys**

1. My coach wants me to throw harder, jump higher, and ________.
   a. run faster
   b. be the fastest runner on the team
   c. thinks I should speed up

2. A new federal program gives students the chance to take several classes this summer and ________.
   a. earning their degrees in as few as two years
   b. earn their degrees in as few as two years
   c. in as few as two years they can earn their degrees

3. French Gothic architecture is defined by its use of flying buttresses, rib vaults, and ________.
   a. decorative elements like sculpture and stained glass
   b. decorating with elements like sculpture and stained glass
   c. of decorative elements like sculpture and stained glass

4. Thomas's doctor recommended that he either go to bed earlier or ________.

   a. that he wake up later

   b. he wake up later

   c. wake up later

5. As she accepted the Nobel Prize, the scientist thanked two groups of people: the colleagues who had supported her research, and ________.

   a. her family, who encouraged her to pursue science when she was young

   b. the family encouraging her to pursue science when she was young

   c. the family members who had encouraged her to pursue science when she was young

## Exercise 22-c
# Parallelism (Editing paragraphs)

To read about this topic, see the section on parallelism in your handbook.

Edit the following paragraph to correct faulty parallelism. The first revision has been done for you.

We all go to college for different reasons: to get an education, ~~because we want~~ to meet new people, and to gain the skills for a job. The best programs reach several of these goals at the same time. I like to take courses that both interest me and building my skills that will lead to a job. It is great to learn about something in class and then I can apply it in a practical situation. Wanting to apply what I learn is why I am doing an internship. I have the opportunity to gain credits, professional skills, and to make important contacts all at the same time. I feel safer starting my career early than to wait until after graduation.

I am a computer science major, so I am interning at a tech company. At first, my internship duties were just the basics: making copies, answering the phone, and I had to file some papers. However, I would often either shadow my supervisor as she attended meetings or assisted her in higher-level duties. As time went on, she taught me how to use the company's systems, how she accomplished her daily tasks, and basic coding. After a few weeks, I was both taking on more exciting projects and was learning new skills.

PART 4

# CHAPTER 23

# Misplaced and dangling modifiers

## Exercise 23-a

## Misplaced and dangling modifiers (Editing sentences)

To read about this topic, see the section on misplaced and dangling modifiers in your handbook.

Circle the letter of the more effective sentence in each pair. Example:

**a. After recovering from the flu, a new job was my first priority.**

**(b.) After recovering from the flu, I made finding a new job my first priority.**

1. a. The president met with the ambassador who had flown in from Singapore in the Oval Office that evening.

   b. That evening in the Oval Office, the president met with the ambassador who had flown in from Singapore.

2. a. If you only wanted fries, you shouldn't have ordered the milkshake too.

   b. If you wanted only fries, you shouldn't have ordered the milkshake too.

3. a. Not all journalists are news reporters; some write opinion columns or reviews.

   b. All journalists are not news reporters; some write opinion columns or reviews.

4. a. While reading a book on my Kindle, the battery went dead.

   b. While I was reading a book on my Kindle, its battery went dead.

5. a. Marie Curie was only the person who won the Nobel Prize in two fields of science and the first woman who won one at all.

   b. Marie Curie was the only person who won the Nobel Prize in two fields of science and the first woman who won one at all.

# Exercise 23-b
## Misplaced and dangling modifiers (Editing sentences)

To read about this topic, see the section on misplaced and dangling modifiers in your handbook.

Edit the following sentences to eliminate misplaced, awkwardly placed, and dangling modifiers. Example:

> ~~After so many accidents occurred on it,~~ T/he chicken decided never to cross the road again/ *after so many accidents occurred on the road.*

1. Just adding one or two sentences to the report will add much more detail.
2. The story goes that H. J. Heinz started out at people's doorsteps selling homemade horseradish.
3. After acting so rudely, we left the party disgusted by the host's immature behavior.
4. You have to usually make an account before you can post a comment to an online forum.
5. While riding a bike to school, a car almost hit Carlos.

## Exercise 23-c
# Misplaced and dangling modifiers (Editing paragraphs)

To read about this topic, see the section on misplaced and dangling modifiers in your handbook.

Edit the following paragraph to eliminate misplaced, awkwardly placed, and dangling modifiers. The first revision has been done for you.

**While ^Jenna was studying for her final, fatigue set in. Jenna only had one exam left, but it was for her least favorite course: economics. She had been surprised to discover how much in this class she struggled. The problem might have been overconfidence. Having done well in previous business-related courses, economics had seemed familiar and manageable at first. She had discovered that economics did not overlap as much as she'd thought after a few weeks with other business courses. Studying for the final, she had reached the point where she was rereading just notes and textbooks without understanding the material. A walk seemed like a good idea to the coffee shop.**

**When she arrived, the coffee shop was quiet. Jenna got a latte. Tasting warm and sweet, she thought the latte was delicious. She spread out her notes and textbooks and started to read again on the table. The change in environment seemed to help. Sixty minutes passed before Jenna knew it. She felt as if she'd gotten more studying done in that one hour than in the previous five hours at the coffee shop.**

PART 4

# CHAPTER 24

# Sentence variety

## Exercise 24-a

## Sentence variety (Editing sentences)

To read about this topic, see the section on sentence variety in your handbook.

Each of the following sentences has the same structure. Rewrite them in different ways, using varied openings and structures. You may need to change other parts of each sentence as well. Example:

> *Because* ^ **Sam was late to work/, ~~Sam~~** *she* ^ **missed the team meeting.**

1. My professor asked us to read stories by Flannery O'Connor; this author is from the South.

2. The refrigerator is full of vegetables; I want fruit.

3. Theodore Roosevelt was a popular leader and politician; nature and the wilderness were his true passions.

4. Xavier was born in California; New York is his true home.

5. She worked at the library during the day; she attended courses in the evenings.

## Exercise 24-b
# Sentence variety (Editing sentences)

To read about this topic, see the section on sentence variety in your handbook.

Edit each of the following sentences in two ways, to provide varied openings and structures. You may need to change other parts of each sentence as well. Example:

> *who*
> a. **My brother, ^ is an avid hiker, ~~and he~~ told us about his adventures.**
>
> *An avid hiker, my*
> b. **^ ~~My~~ brother ~~is an avid hiker, and he~~ told us about his adventures.**

1. a. Florence Nightingale was a famous nurse, a writer, and a social reformer.
   b. Florence Nightingale was a famous nurse, a writer, and a social reformer.

2. a. Tenskwatawa was an important Native American leader who encouraged his people to give up alcohol along with European clothing and tools.
   b. Tenskwatawa was an important Native American leader who encouraged his people to give up alcohol along with European clothing and tools.

3. a. My mother is a smart shopper, and she managed to find the shoes she wanted at a lower price at a different store even though the sale had ended.
   b. My mother is a smart shopper, and she managed to find the shoes she wanted at a lower price at a different store even though the sale had ended.

4. a. Graham was fixing his bike and Betty was washing her car this morning.
   b. Graham was fixing his bike and Betty was washing her car this morning.

5. a. The Rhone River and the Rhine River both rise out of the Alps of Switzerland, and are known for their beautiful landscapes.
   b. The Rhone River and the Rhine River both rise out of the Alps of Switzerland, and are known for their beautiful landscapes.

## Exercise 24-c
# Sentence variety (Editing paragraphs)

To read about this topic, see the section on sentence variety in your handbook.

The following paragraphs are grammatically correct but dull. Revise them to add variety. You may need to combine some sentences. The first revision has been done for you.

Discovered in 1801, the
~~The~~ first minor planet was ~~discovered in 1801. It was~~ called Ceres. A minor planet orbits a sun. It is neither a planet nor a comet. Over 600,000 minor planets have been registered since then. The Minor Planet Center is in Northeastern America. It handles hundreds of requests each year to officially recognize and name celestial objects.

The names used to come primarily from Greek and Roman mythology. The minor planet Hermes is one. Popular music often provides a source of naming now. Five objects are named after the 1960s band the Beatles. There is a minor planet Beatles named after the whole band. Each group member has a minor planet named after him. Ringo Starr is the band's drummer. He has the minor planet Starr named after him. It isn't a star. It is just a minor planet about five miles in diameter. Other minor planets are named after bands such as Yes and ZZ Top. Maybe one day there will be a minor planet named Lady Gaga.

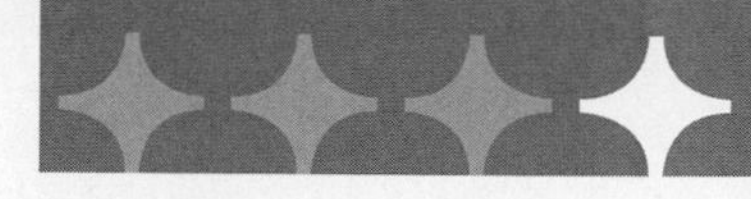



# CHAPTER 25

# Sentence fragments

## Exercise 25-a
## Sentence fragments (Editing sentences)

To read about this topic, see the section on fragments in your handbook.

Each of the following word groups combines one sentence and one fragment. Identify the fragment, then edit by attaching it to the existing sentence or rewriting it as a complete sentence. Example:

> **Not long ago, there was only one kind of eating apple that you could buy/, ~~The~~ *the* Red Delicious.**

1. Because the Red Delicious apple variety stayed ripe for a long time. Growers loved it.

2. Growers kept changing the Red Delicious variety over the years. Making the apples redder and even more long-lasting.

3. Unfortunately, there was a negative side effect to their changes. Specifically, tasting worse.

4. Apple researchers in Japan developed the Fuji apple. Using our old friend the Red Delicious.

5. The researchers who developed the apple gave it a name. *Fuji* after the name of their research station.

## Exercise 25-b

# Sentence fragments (Editing sentences)

To read about this topic, see the section on fragments in your handbook.

In each of the following pairs, one word group is a complete sentence and one word group contains a fragment. Circle the letter of the complete sentence in each pairing. Example:

**(a.) The Florida Keys are actually hundreds of little islands.**

**b. Little islands running from the mainland to Key West.**

1. a. Since the bigger keys end at Key West.

   b. Key West is the westernmost of the bigger keys.

2. a. The road to Key West is a series of bridges.

   b. The bridges which span from key to key.

3. a. Although the bridges were built on a previously existing causeway, they are fairly new.

   b. Although the causeway was built on the remains of an abandoned railway line.

4. a. Building the railway line, a difficult task.

   b. Striking hurricanes are common in the keys.

5. a. However, what doomed the railway was a different problem.

   b. The problem being lack of docking facilities on Key West.

## Exercise 25-c

# Sentence fragments (Editing paragraphs)

To read about this topic, see the section on fragments in your handbook.

Edit the following paragraph to eliminate sentence fragments. The first revision has been done for you.

Key West is the southernmost city in the continental United States~~.~~, ~~Just~~ just barely above the Tropic of Cancer. In fact, Key West is nearly as far south as Hawaii. A fact that surprises many people. It is interesting to see how alike and unlike Key West and Hawaii are. Although they are so close. They are quite different physically. Key West is a set of coral islands lying in a shallow coral sea. Hawaii, on the other hand, is a set of separate islands perched on the tops of gigantic volcanic mountains. Rising abruptly out of very deep water. Key West is surrounded by other islands and is only a short distance from the Florida mainland. A mere seventy miles. Cuba is close by too. Only ninety miles south of Key West. Hawaii, by comparison, is one of the most physically isolated places. In the entire world. The native plants and animals in Key West and Hawaii, very different too. Virtually every plant and animal in Key West is also found everywhere else in the Caribbean. Hawaii's isolation meant that the original stock of plants and animals was extremely limited. The few things that did get to Hawaii diversified and specialized in amazing ways. Since they had so little competition from other species. As a result, many plants and animals in Hawaii are found nowhere else in the world.

# CHAPTER 26

# Run-on sentences

## Exercise 26-a

## Run-on sentences (Editing sentences)

To read about this topic, see the section on run-on sentences in your handbook.

Revise each of the following run-on sentences using two different methods. Example:

a. **My parents had three dogs, ^but I always secretly wanted a cat.**

b. **~~My~~ ^Although my parents had three dogs, I always secretly wanted a cat.**

1. a. She had to stay up late last night, this morning she is sleeping in.

   b. She had to stay up late last night, this morning she is sleeping in.

2. a. Trying to sell a house in this economic climate is tough, nobody can get a loan.

   b. Trying to sell a house in this economic climate is tough, nobody can get a loan.

3. a. Elizabeth Cochrane Seaman was a pioneering investigative reporter she was better known by her pen name Nellie Bly.

   b. Elizabeth Cochrane Seaman was a pioneering investigative reporter she was better known by her pen name Nellie Bly.

4. a. He had two competing desires, he wanted to make it to class on time, but he wanted to go back to sleep.

   b. He had two competing desires, he wanted to make it to class on time, but he wanted to go back to sleep.

5. a. Cheetahs are one of the lightest big cat species, they are also the fastest.

   b. Cheetahs are one of the lightest big cat species, they are also the fastest.

## Exercise 26-b
# Run-on sentences (Editing sentences)

To read about this topic, see the section on run-on sentences in your handbook.

Some of the following word groups are run-on sentences. If a sentence is run-on, revise it using a suitable revision strategy. If a sentence is correct, mark it as "correct." Example:

**When**
**I took a class on Native American literature, I first became interested in Janet**
**^ ^**
**Campbell Hale's writing.**

1. When I slipped on the ice while going to work, I wrenched my left knee.

2. What's wrong with the car it keeps making a grinding noise.

3. W. E. B. Du Bois led the Niagara Movement, it was a civil rights group founded in 1905.

4. He is going back to school as soon as he saves enough money.

5. Hilda Solis was a congresswoman, she later became the Secretary of Labor.

# Exercise 26-c
## Run-on sentences (Editing paragraphs)

To read about this topic, see the section on run-on sentences in your handbook.

Revise each run-on sentence in the following paragraph. The first sentence has been revised for you.

**Parking at the school has always been difficult, but it seems to be getting worse every year. There are always more students, there is never any more parking. Like a lot of urban schools, the campus is relatively small in proportion to the number of students this naturally causes a lot of problems for parking. To begin with, full-time staff and faculty get half of the existing parking the other half is for two-hour parking meters, which are always full. There is actually a fair amount of street parking near the campus, the problem is that it is first come, first served. If you have afternoon labs or a late meeting, all the spaces are long gone by the time you get to school. There is no way to tell how much time it will take to find a parking place, it could be a few minutes or a half hour. Fortunately, the campus is in a good neighborhood students and faculty do not have to worry about safety when walking to their cars, even after dark. The one bit of good news is that the school is in the process of buying a large vacant parking lot a couple of miles from campus. The school will then charter some buses it can run a continuous shuttle from the parking lot to campus. This change can't come soon enough.**

# CHAPTER 27
# Subject-verb agreement

## Exercise 27-a
## Subject-verb agreement (Editing sentences)

To read about this topic, see the section on subject-verb agreement in your handbook.

In the following sentences, the verb is in italic type. Find and underline the simple subject to which the verb refers, and make the verb agree with it. If the form of the verb is correct, write "OK" above it. Example:

> **The suggestions about cutting the budget always ~~seems~~ [seem] terribly simplistic.**

1. The integration of so many different ideas *take* a lot of time and effort.
2. The ranking of all the qualifying teams *are* always controversial.
3. Examination of the documents clearly *shows* that the defendant is innocent.
4. Everyone on the team is *worried* about losing the game.
5. One of the trees in our neighborhood *have crashed* down onto the power line.

## Exercise 27-b
# Subject-verb agreement (Editing sentences)

To read about this topic, see the section on subject-verb agreement in your handbook.

Each of the following sentences has a compound subject. Underline the compound subject and correct the verb. If the verb is correct, write "OK" above it. Example:

> *have*
> **A hamburger, fries, and a Coke ~~has~~ ^ been my normal lunch for years.**

1. During the summer, the thunder and the lightning in our area is just amazing.

2. The light in the garage and the light over the sink needs replacing.

3. What "football" means in America and what it means in the rest of the world are totally different things.

4. Loud drums, thunderclaps, and even our doorbell frightens my little sister.

5. The characters and the plot of his latest book is just like those in all his other books.

## Exercise 27-c
# Subject-verb agreement (Editing paragraphs)

To read about this topic, see the section on subject-verb agreement in your handbook.

Circle the correct verb from each pair of verbs in parentheses. The first selection has been made for you.

All products containing chocolate in any form (comes / come) from the seeds of the cacao tree. The Mayas in Central America (was / were) the first to discover how to produce chocolate from cacao seeds. A number of large, melon-shaped pods (grows / grow) directly on the trunk and larger branches of the cacao tree. Each of these pods (contains / contain) up to forty almond-shaped seeds. The seeds, after being removed from the pod, fermented, and dried, (is / are) transformed into the commercial cocoa bean.

The first step in producing chocolate from the cacao beans (is / are) to remove the outer shells. What remains after the shells have been removed (is / are) called nibs. Nibs contain a high percentage of a natural fat called cocoa butter. When heated and ground, the nibs (releases / release) cocoa butter. The mixture of cocoa butter and finely ground nibs (forms / form) a liquid called chocolate liquor. The chocolate liquor, after being cooled and molded into little cakes, (is / are) what we know as baking chocolate. Baking chocolate and sugar (is / are) at the heart of all those wonderful chocolate goodies that almost everyone (loves / love).

# CHAPTER 28

# Pronoun reference

## Exercise 28-a

## Pronoun reference (Editing sentences)

To read about this topic, see the section on pronoun reference in your handbook.

In each of the following sentences, the vague or faulty pronoun is underlined. Replace the pronoun or revise the sentence. Example:

**Climate change has gotten caught up in politics. This ^politicizing is what scientists were afraid of.**

1. We did not hear about the proposal, so we need to talk about that.
2. The street is full of striking employees which are protesting low pay and poor benefits.
3. The weather forecast did not predict the storm. The coast suffered a lot of damage because of this.
4. The governor and the legislature are virtually at war with each other, which has brought the state to its knees.
5. San Francisco is one of the most photographed cities in the world. This makes it a natural tourist destination.

## Exercise 28-b
# Pronoun reference (Editing sentences)

To read about this topic, see the section on pronoun reference in your handbook.

In the following sentences, find the faulty pronoun references and fix them. If a sentence is correct, mark it as "correct." Example:

All
**~~In all~~ of the reports/ ~~they~~ claimed the new drug was the most effective at treating strep throat.**

1. In 1930, Pluto was declared a planet. It was reclassified as a dwarf planet in 2006.
2. All of the candidates which were in the running were shocked by the results, even the candidate who won.
3. My roommate met an old friend recently. She is going to law school now.
4. Besides bringing a shovel, Dalit brought food for us to eat on our camping trip. We might not need it, but the food will come in handy.
5. In his speech, Louis argued that the best way to increase involvement in student government is to give a tuition break to members of the student senate. That happened last week.

## Exercise 28-c
# Pronoun reference (Editing paragraphs)

To read about this topic, see the section on pronoun reference in your handbook.

Edit the following paragraphs to correct errors in pronoun reference. The first revision has been done for you.

"Star Wars" was the nickname of a US military program/. The name ~~which~~ came from the popular sci-fi film series. It was a large research program designed to provide military defense in outer space. This was initiated by the president in the 1980s, which at the time was Ronald Reagan. It was the height of the cold war. The national defense strategy at the time was "mutually assured destruction." This basically means that when two sides have nuclear weapons, they both won't use them. For the president, he thought this strategy wouldn't work and wanted a better defense system.

Although it had the official title of "Strategic Defense Initiative," the public never embraced that as much as the catchier title "Star Wars." It was initially an insult from Senator Ted Kennedy, which meant to make fun of the initiative. However, the name stuck. In the Department of Defense, they researched and developed "Star Wars" throughout the 1980s. That was heavily funded for years. However, it underwent major cutbacks once the cold war ended. It ended officially in 1993.

# CHAPTER 29

# Pronoun and noun case

## Exercise 29-a

## Pronoun and noun case (Editing sentences)

To read about this topic, see the section on pronoun and noun case in your handbook.

Edit the following sentences so that there are no errors in pronoun or noun case. Example:

> **My grandmother told me a story about ~~she~~ her and her friends sneaking into movie theaters when they were young girls.**

1. Our cousins visit San Juan often; last year us and them made the trip together.

2. The two most vocal women, Shandra and me, were asked to petition the mayor.

3. In the review session, the TA did a sample problem for my lab partner and I.

4. Me and the other interns gave a presentation at the planning meeting.

5. The problem is the government characterizing immigrants as criminals.

## Exercise 29-b
# Pronoun and noun case (Editing sentences)

To read about this topic, see the section on pronoun and noun case in your handbook.

Edit the following sentences so that there are no errors in pronoun or noun case. If the sentence is correct, mark it as "correct." Example:

> **Juan and ~~her~~ ^she^ will be leaving for New Orleans soon.**

1. Her and her little dog returned to Kansas.
2. It was them, not the mayor, who finally raised the money to repair the bridge.
3. Frida Kahlo and her husband, Diego Rivera, were both painters; he and his work were wider known at the time, but it was she who became well-known and influential after their deaths.
4. Did he ever figure out what they should have said to she?
5. They ordered it especially for my mother and I.

## Exercise 29-c
# Pronoun and noun case (Editing paragraphs)

To read about this topic, see the section on pronoun and noun case in your handbook.

Some of the personal pronouns in this passage are italicized; some of the italicized words are not in the correct case. Find and replace the incorrect pronouns. The first one has been corrected for you.

**When I was in high school, my father and ~~*me*~~ I would build a new house every other summer. My father and mother were teachers, so *him* and *her* always had summers off. During the first summer, my father and *me* would pour the foundation and do the framing and roofing. During the school year, a general contractor would supervise the plumbing, wiring, and other specialties. The following summer, my father and *I* would finish the interior work. During the next school year, my mother would take charge of all the interior decoration, and then *her* would put the house on the market.**

**When you build a house, much of the work is actually done by specialized subcontractors: plumbers, electricians, plasterers, woodworkers, tilers, and so on. Convenience is part of the reason we work with our general contractor, Richard. It is *him* who hires specialists for each house. He works with many subcontractors, so *he* knows which of *they* are available, do the best work, and have the experience. My father and I can focus on the building and rely on *he* to find the specialists.**

# CHAPTER 30

# Verbs

## Exercise 30-a
## Verbs (Editing sentences)

To read about this topic, see the sections on verbs in your handbook.

Each of the sentences below contains two underlined verbs. Correct verbs with missing *–ed* and *–s* endings and incorrect forms of irregular verbs. If the verb is correct, write "OK." Example:

> **This past Christmas, we ~~goed~~ *went* to Chicago, where my parents live *OK*.**

1. I leaved my towel in the locker that be nearest the door.

2. The fact that Hawaii do not go on daylight savings time always confuse people.

3. I usually check my e-mail as soon as I got back from lunch.

4. Yesterday he deposits the money in an account that he keeps at the local credit union.

5. The accident occur on a stretch of road that have a reputation for being dangerous.

## Exercise 30-b
# Verbs (Editing sentences)

To read about this topic, see the sections on verbs in your handbook.

For each sentence, choose the verb form that best completes the sentence. Example:

**Headlights that stay on all the time __________ significantly reduced car accidents.**

**a. has**

**(b.) have**

**c. had**

1. After the book __________ a big hit in Europe, American publishers were willing to take a chance on it.

   a. becomes

   b. became

   c. become

2. After I finished assembling the bike, I __________ a leftover part.

   a. finded

   b. find

   c. found

3. Artists today are still influenced by the art styles that __________ in prewar Germany.

   a. originated

   b. originate

   c. had originate

4. Yertle's car ___________ down just outside of Atlanta.

   a. breaked

   b. broked

   c. broke

5. Young people ___________ buying landline phones less and less often these days.

   a. are

   b. were

   c. be

# Exercise 30-c
## Verbs (Editing paragraphs)

To read about this topic, see the sections on verbs in your handbook.

Edit the following paragraph to correct problems with –s and –*ed* verb forms and irregular verbs. The first correction has been done for you.

**Provence is a region in the southeast corner of France, which** *borders* **~~bordered~~ Italy. The name Provence referred to the fact that it was the first province created by the ancient Romans outside the Italian peninsula. Today, Provence still contained an amazing number of well-preserved Roman ruins. The beautiful beach and Mediterranean Sea runs along the region. The largest and best-known city in Provence is Marseille. The ancient Greeks and Romans call it Massalia, and use it as an important port and trading post. Now, Marseille remained a center of commerce for France and all of Europe. While a few other big towns exists on the coast, Provence was still famous for its wild country and beautiful scenery. Provence be especially known for its abundance of wildflowers in the spring. These flowers is use to make some of the world's most expensive perfumes.**

# CHAPTER 31

# Articles

## Exercise 31-a

## Articles (Editing sentences)

To read about this topic, see the section on articles in your handbook.

Fill in the blanks with an appropriate article. Example:

**We had to put ___the___ furniture in storage while we were away.**

1. They need to find __________ better source of raw materials.

2. You have __________ visitor.

3. Please put away __________ tools that you have taken out.

4. The storm completely eroded away __________ exposed beaches.

5. Some people don't have __________ imagination.

## Exercise 31-b
# Articles (Editing sentences)

To read about this topic, see the section on articles in your handbook.

Edit the following sentences for errors in the use of articles. If a sentence is correct, mark it as "correct." Example:

**The company was hoping for ^a more favorable trend.**

1. There was a confusion about an instructions.

2. Airports have become hubs for economic development.

3. Most countries tax the cigarettes and the alcohol heavily.

4. We don't have training we need to fix computer.

5. Most of nonprofit organizations I know are dedicated to the great cause.

# Exercise 31-c
## Articles (Editing paragraphs)

To read about this topic, see the section on articles in your handbook.

Edit the following paragraph for errors in the use of articles. The first correction has been done for you.

**When I was ^a young child, sports were only available through the schools. That meant that during a summer, children had no access to an organized sports when they actually had a free time to do them. Situation is different for the children today. Big problem for them is having so many options that they don't know what to pick. Should children play Little League baseball, should they do the tennis at Parks and Recreation, or should they take swimming lessons at the YMCA? Should they take a karate, or should they take a tae kwon do? It sometimes seems that children today are lost in sea of options, making it easy to flit from sport to another without getting very good at one of them. Maybe it is not so critical with an individual sports or martial arts because they can be started up again without too much loss of skills. On sport team it is totally different matter because it takes long time to build team spirit or a teamwork.**

# CHAPTER 32

# Commas and unnecessary commas

## Exercise 32-a

## Commas and unnecessary commas (Editing sentences)

To read about this topic, see the sections on the comma in your handbook.

In each of the following sentences, find where the comma(s) should be and add it to the sentence. If a sentence does not need a comma, mark it as "correct." Example:

> **In the Middle Eastern country of Yemen, which is where my parents were married, a wedding feast can last as long as three weeks.**

1. Pulitzer Prize winner Toni Morrison who passed away in 2019 wrote about important themes like the African American experience and female identity.

2. Most people are terrified of being bitten by a shark yet far more people are injured each year by dogs than sharks.

3. Bahir is dropping by my apartment later so I suppose I should pick up my dirty clothes and wash the dishes.

4. Leonardo da Vinci was not only an artist but also a prolific inventor.

5. On my birthday I am going to see my favorite singer Elton John.

## Exercise 32-b

# Commas and unnecessary commas (Editing sentences)

To read about this topic, see the sections on the comma in your handbook.

Three of the following sentences have unnecessary commas. Find them and cross them out. If a sentence does not have an unnecessary comma, mark it as "correct." Example:

**My grocery list includes/ milk, eggs, and celery.**

1. To keep people from sneaking up on him, folk hero, Wild Bill Hickok, placed crumpled newspapers around his bed.
2. The test will cover several subjects, including but not limited to the Great Depression, World War II, and the Cold War.
3. Although Wally Amos is best known for his brand of cookies, he was also the first African American talent agent, for the William Morris Agency.
4. Someone called for you this morning, and left a strange message.
5. I enjoy eating strawberries, blueberries, and blackberries, but for some reason, I have never liked raspberries.

## Exercise 32-c

# Commas and unnecessary commas (Editing paragraphs)

To read about this topic, see the sections on the comma in your handbook.

Edit the following paragraph by adding commas where they are needed and removing unnecessary commas. The first revision has been done for you.

The first true clocks were built in the thirteenth century, an era when accurate timekeeping became increasingly important. There were some existing timekeeping devices such as, sundials. However these were often used in situations, that were not ideal. Sundials were useless at night, when there was insufficient light for casting a shadow. The wind could blow out candles which also could be used to estimate the time. The timekeeping devices, that used streams, could freeze in winter. By the thirteenth century the European monastery was a major social organization, that depended on precise accurate and reliable timing. The monks' cooperative work efforts required them to coordinate their duties, in terms of timing. This was an important need that called for a machine that could keep reliable time. Because of this the modern clock was devised.

# CHAPTER 33
# Apostrophes

## Exercise 33-a
## Apostrophes (Editing sentences)

To read about this topic, see the section on the apostrophe in your handbook.

Each of the following sentences has multiple apostrophes. One of the apostrophes is used incorrectly. Delete or move the incorrect apostrophe. Example:

**At least ten Kennedy's have been elected to one of America's public offices.**

1. I have three essays to complete for my women's studies' class.

2. Alfred Wegner's degree's were in astronomy, but his life's work was in meteorology.

3. A starfish's eyes are located at the tips of each of it's arms.

4. Hold the acid at arm's length and make sure you're wearing your safety goggle's.

5. Sheila was'nt aware that her parents' new house was so big.

## Exercise 33-b
# Apostrophes (Editing sentences)

To read about this topic, see the section on the apostrophe in your handbook.

None of the sentences below have apostrophes. Add any that are needed and make any necessary corrections in spelling. If a sentence is correct, mark it as "correct." Example:

**The guppy's name comes from the name of the man ~~whose~~ who's responsible for discovering the species.**

1. Heres a fun fact: the saxophones inventor was named Adolphe Sax.
2. If we arent out the door in five minutes, were going to be late for the Johnsons anniversary party.
3. The drivers of all four cars almost crashed when their tires slid on the ice.
4. Im not a fan of coffee, but your welcome to have as many cups as you want.
5. It isnt Floridas high temperature thats so suffocating; its its humidity.

# Exercise 33-c
# Apostrophes (Editing paragraphs)

To read about this topic, see the section on the apostrophe in your handbook.

In the following paragraphs, add apostrophes where they are missing and delete or correct them where they are misused. The first revision has been done for you.

The word *parasite* comes from a Greek word meaning a person who doesn’t do honest work but depends entirely on wealthy and powerful patrons handout’s. Biologist’s adopted the term to describe a huge variety of creature’s that steal their nourishment from hosts, often causing their hosts death. For many animals, its just the way they have to survive. However, the behavior of parasites’ strikes most humans as vicious and ugly. It is’nt a surprise that their behavior has captured many writer’s and filmmaker’s imaginations.

One of the best fictional depictions of parasites is in the science fiction movie *Alien*. In that movie, a spaceships crew discovers small aliens that attack someones’ neck. Later, a creature pierces through the man’s stomach and leaps out. The alien laid an egg in he’s abdomen; the eggs hatched and chewed through he’s intestines. This horrible scenario is actually based on the real behavior of parasitic wasps’. They lay they’re eggs in living caterpillars. As the eggs mature, they eat the internal organ’s of the caterpillar, sparing only the organs necessary to keep the caterpillar alive. When the eggs are fully mature, they erupt through the caterpillars skin, leaving behind their hollowed-out hosts’ body.

# CHAPTER 34

# Quotation marks

## Exercise 34-a
## Quotation marks (Editing sentences)

To read about this topic, see the section on quotation marks in your handbook.

Edit the following sentences to correct the use of quotation marks and of other punctuation with quotation marks. Example:

**Who wrote "Letter from Birmingham Jail?" ?**

1. Gage asked. "When can we eat?"

2. "The store opens at ten, she said, but the deli won't open until eleven."

3. "Mary Shelley wrote, "Nothing is so painful to the human mind as a great and sudden change."" the speaker told the lecture attendees.

4. "Watch out for that tree" the lumberjack shouted!

5. I have a hard time understanding the plot of the story "An Occurrence at Owl Creek Bridge", yet my essay on it is due soon.

## Exercise 34-b
# Quotation marks (Editing sentences)

To read about this topic, see the section on quotation marks in your handbook.

Four of the following sentences need quotation marks. Insert the quotation marks in the correct places. Mark the sentence that does not need quotation marks as "correct." Example:

**Bjorg asked, "Do you want to play tennis?"**

1. The British singer Adele said that one of her favorite songs to perform was Rolling in the Deep.

2. When describing the song, she said, it's a dark bluesy gospel disco tune.

3. Are you still writing a paper about Langston Hughes's poem I, Too, Sing America?

4. The reporter asked the governor to comment on the accusations, but the governor claimed that he had nothing to say.

5. The sign read Keep Out, but I asked myself, Who would mind if I went in?

## Exercise 34-c
# Quotation marks (Editing paragraphs)

To read about this topic, see the section on quotation marks in your handbook.

Edit the following paragraphs to correct the use of quotation marks and of punctuation with quotation marks. The first correction has been made for you.

Literary works have long served as a basis for lyrics used in popular music, including classic rock hits such as Led Zeppelin's "Ramble On." That song makes references to Tolkien's *Lord of the Rings*. One line mentions the "darkest depths of Mordor", and another refers to an evil being named "Gollum". Have you seen the music video for the country song "If I Die Young?" It shows a member of The Band Perry holding a book containing Alfred, Lord Tennyson's poem The Lady of Shalott, which influenced the song's story. "Sink me in the river at dawn, the vocalist sings, send me away with the words of a love song.". This is a reference to the ending of the poem. A tune by the Indigo Girls, "Left Me a Fool," refers to the same poem. They even mention it by name, singing, You remind me of Shalott / Only made of shadows even though you're not.

Lana Del Rey, who has won many musical awards, mentions Nabokov's novel *Lolita* in "Off to the Races"; at one point she sings. "I said, "Hon' you never looked so beautiful / As you do now my man."" Several of her other songs make references to poets Walt Whitman and Allen Ginsberg. Even heavy metal bands have gotten into the act. For instance, the band "Avenged Sevenfold" took its name from the famous biblical story of Cain and Abel. The fourth chapter of the book of Genesis indicates Cain's death would be "avenged sevenfold".

# Answers to exercises

**Exercise 15-a, page 147** *Possible answers:*

1. An analysis of superhero films focused on male characters, with parenting as a theme. A possible audience is superhero film enthusiasts or film study scholars.
2. A cause-and-effect look at how reports of animal disease in news outlets affect consumer demand for meat products. The audience is probably a general audience.
3. An informative article aimed at experts—counselors who work in a school setting and see students who harm themselves or are thinking about doing so.

**Exercise 15-b, page 149**

1. Illustration. A general statement about black officials' responses to black crime is followed by examples of different responses.
2. Comparison and contrast. The writer compares and contrasts the responsibilities of two government agencies that regulate dietary supplements.

**Exercise 15-c, page 151** *Possible answer:*

*Modicum* means "small amount." The clue is the phrase *low-cost, low-effort* earlier in the sentence.

**Exercise 15-d, page 152**

Answers will vary.

**Exercise 15-e, page 154**

Answers will vary.

**Exercise 15-f, page 156**

Answers will vary.

**Exercise 16-a, page 157**

1. b; a is a question.
2. b; a is a fact and not debatable.
3. a; b is a fact and not debatable.
4. a; b is a fact and not debatable.
5. a; b is too general for a college paper.
6. a; b is too vague for an argument.
7. b; a is too general for a college paper.
8. a; b is both too general and too factual.

**Exercise 16-b, page 161** *Possible answer:*

Investing in digital health monitoring is the best way for today's health care providers to promote patients' well-being and confidence in caregivers and, at the same time, lower their own costs in the long run.

**Exercise 16-c, page 163**

Answers will vary.

**Exercise 17-a, page 168**

1. a
2. c

**Exercise 17-b, page 170** *Possible answers:*

1. Taking a midday nap can have benefits unrecognized by many people.
2. Afghan girls still face many obstacles to attending school, despite work by education advocates.

**Exercise 17-c, page 171**

Answer will vary.

**Exercise 18-a, page 173**

1. Plagiarized. The student uses some exact words and phrases from the source (*intimate, broken into discrete bits*) without enclosing them in quotation marks and also mimics the structure of the source. The student also has not cited the source in a signal phrase or in parentheses.
2. OK. The student has correctly enclosed the exact words of the source in quotation marks and has used brackets for a word added to fit the surrounding sentence.
3. OK. The student has correctly enclosed the exact words of the source in quotation marks.
4. OK. The student has correctly paraphrased the source without using the language or structure of the source.
5. Plagiarized. The student has put quotation marks around exact words from the source but has failed to cite the author of the source in a signal phrase or in parentheses.

**Exercise 18-b, page 175**

1. Plagiarized. The student uses some exact words and phrases from the source (*spend more time thinking and talking about other people than . . . anything else*) without enclosing them in quotation marks and also mimics the structure of the source. The student also has not cited the source in a signal phrase or in parentheses.
2. OK. The student has correctly enclosed the exact words of the source in quotation marks and has cited the source of the quotation in parentheses.
3. OK. The student has correctly enclosed the exact words of the source in quotation marks and has cited the source of the quotations in a signal phrase and in parentheses.
4. Plagiarized. The student has put exact words from the source in quotation marks but has omitted the words *briefly but* after *themselves* without using an ellipsis to indicate missing words.
5. OK. The student has paraphrased the source's ideas without using the exact words or structure of the source and has cited the source in a signal phrase and in parentheses.

**Exercise 18-c, page 177**

1. Common knowledge. Yoknapatawpha County is mentioned in virtually all sources discussing Faulkner, so his invention of this place can be considered common knowledge.
2. Needs citation. The scholar whose research led to this hypothesis should be given credit.
3. Common knowledge. Information about birth and death dates and the life circumstances of well-known authors usually does not require citation.
4. Needs citation. A reader would not encounter this information repeatedly in books and articles on Shakespeare, so it requires a citation.
5. Needs citation. This information might be considered controversial, especially among admirers of Disney.
6. Common knowledge. This is information that would appear in many sources on Wordsworth and Shelley, so a paper on these poets would not need to cite it.
7. Needs citation. Statistics generally require a citation.
8. Common knowledge. This is a definition of a standard literary form — a type of information found in almost any introductory literature text.
9. Common knowledge. This information about Iris Murdoch is widely known, and a student would find mention of it in most recent sources related to Murdoch.

10. Needs citation. This information would probably be surprising to many readers (and some might doubt its truthfulness), so a citation is needed.

**Exercise 18-d, page 179**

1. This sentence is unacceptable. The second part of the sentence is a direct quotation from the source, so it must appear in quotation marks:

   Wind power accounts for more than 1% of California's electricity, reports Frederic Golden, and "[d]uring breezy early mornings in summer, the contribution goes even higher" (B1).
2. OK. Quoted words appear in quotation marks, and the student provides the author's name in the signal phrase and the page number in parentheses.
3. This sentence is unacceptable. The words appearing in quotation marks are not word-for word accurate. Also, the statement is not accurate, because the 8% figure applies only on certain days. The following is an acceptable revision:

   Mary A. Ilyin reports that under certain weather conditions, "the wind accounts for up to 8%" of California's electricity (qtd. in Golden B1).
4. OK. The brackets indicate that the word *California's* does not appear in the original source, and otherwise the quotation is word-for-word accurate. In addition, the MLA citation correctly indicates that the words belong to Ilyin, who was quoted by Golden.
5. This passage is unacceptable. The second sentence is a dropped quotation. Quotations should be introduced with a signal phrase, usually naming the author. The following is an acceptable revision:

   California has pioneered the use of wind power. According to Frederic Golden, "Half of California's turbines . . . are located in Altamont Pass" (B1).

**Exercise 18-e, page 181**

1. OK. The student has put quotation marks around the exact words from the source and has handled the MLA citation correctly, putting the name of the author in a signal phrase and the page number in parentheses.
2. The sentence is unacceptable. The phrase *active safety* is enclosed in quotation marks in the source; single quotation marks are required for a quotation within a quotation. In addition, the student has failed to use an ellipsis mark to indicate that the word *which* is omitted from the quotation. The following is an acceptable revision:

   Gladwell argues that "'active safety' . . . is every bit as important" as a vehicle's ability to withstand a collision (31).
3. This passage is unacceptable. The second sentence is a dropped quotation. Quotations should be introduced with a signal phrase, usually naming the author. The following is an acceptable revision:

   A majority of drivers can, indeed, be wrong. As Malcolm Gladwell points out, "Most of us think that S.U.V.s are much safer than sports cars" (31).
4. OK. The student has introduced the quotation with a signal phrase and used brackets to indicate the change from *you* to *they* to fit the grammar of the sentence.
5. This sentence is unacceptable. The student has changed the wording of the source (*of surviving*) to fit the grammar of the sentence (*to survive*) but has not indicated the change with brackets. The following is an acceptable revision:

   Gladwell explains that most people expect an S.U.V. to survive "a collision with a hypothetical tractor-trailer in the other lane" (31).

**Exercise 18-f, page 183**

1. a. Because Sommers is quoted in an article written by someone else, MLA style requires

the abbreviation *qtd. in* (for *quoted in*) before the author of the article in the in-text citation.

2. b. When the author of a source is given in a signal phrase, the title of the source is not necessary in an in-text citation.
3. b. For a work with three or more authors, only the first author's name is used; *et al.* is used in place of all other names.
4. a. Statistics taken from a source must be cited with author and page number.
5. b. The author's name, not the title of the source, should be used in an in-text citation.
6. a. The exact words of the source are enclosed in quotation marks.
7. b. For an unsigned source, a shortened form of the title is used in the in-text citation.
8. a. When the works cited list includes two or more works by one author, the in-text citation includes a shortened form of the title of the work cited.
9. b. A website with no author should be cited with a shortened form of the title, not with the sponsor of the website.
10. a. When a source has two authors, both authors should be named in the in-text citation.

**Exercise 18-g, page 187**

1. b. An MLA works cited entry for an article with no author begins with the title of the article.
2. b. The terms *volume* and *number* are abbreviated, and the name of the database and the URL for the database home page are included.
3. a. When citing a single work from an anthology, list the individual work first, beginning with its author's name.
4. b. If a newspaper article appears on pages that are not consecutive, the first page number is followed by a plus sign.
5. a. In an MLA works cited entry, the publication date appears after the website title.
6. a. A works cited entry for an interview begins with the name of the person interviewed, not the person who conducted the interview.
7. b. Elements following the title are separated by commas, and *Narrated by* is spelled out.
8. a. The translator's name is given after the title of the work.
9. a. The access date is not given because the website has an update date.
10. b. A work from a website includes the URL for the work.

**Exercise 18-h, page 191**

1. False. A URL is never used in an in-text citation.
2. True. The alphabetical organization helps readers quickly find the source that has been cited in the text.
3. False. A list of works cited must give complete publication information for any sources cited in the paper. In-text citations alone are not sufficient.
4. True. MLA provides an option for placement of the author's name: it can appear in a signal phrase or in parentheses.
5. False. When a work's author is unknown, the work is listed under its title.
6. False. In the works cited list, only the first author's name is given in reverse order (last name first). A second author's name is given in normal order (first name first).
7. True. If the author is named in a signal phrase, it is possible that nothing will appear in parentheses.
8. False. MLA style does not use any abbreviation before the page number in an in-text citation.
9. True. Because more than one work will appear in the works cited list, the title is necessary for identifying the exact work that has been cited. The author's name is not enough.
10. True. When a permalink or a DOI is available, use it in the works cited list.

**Exercise 19-a, page 193**

1. Student A is committing plagiarism. All borrowed language must be in quotation marks and all sources used must be cited.
2. Student B is not committing plagiarism. The writer is seeking advice about how to organize her essay but not using anyone's ideas or language without credit.
3. Student C is committing plagiarism. The student is passing off someone else's work as her own.
4. Student D is committing plagiarism. All borrowed language must be in quotation marks.
5. Student E is committing plagiarism. Writers must cite all sources that they quote from, paraphrase, or summarize.

**Exercise 19-b, page 196**

Answers will vary.

**Exercise 20-a, page 197**

Answers will vary.

**Exercise 20-b, page 200**

Answers will vary.

**Exercise 20-c, page 203**

1. a; b uses exact language from the source without putting that language in quotation marks.
2. a; b uses sentence structure that is too close to the structure used in the original passage.

Bonus: If the author's name is mentioned in a signal phrase within the sentence, there is no need to repeat the author's name in the parentheses.

**Exercise 21-a, p. 205**

1. I used this computer.
2. In Japan, cities provide names only for major streets.
3. France's government bans television advertisements for wine.
4. The college president announced the tuition increase.
5. Vice President Joe Biden made a cameo appearance in a fifth-season episode of *Parks and Recreation*.

**Exercise 21-b, p. 206**

1. Jim prepared supper.
2. Active
3. In 2013, President Obama invited Beyoncé to perform at the presidential inaugural gala.
4. Parker is too embarrassed to tell his manager that he missed the deadline.
5. The recession affected everyone.

**Exercise 21-c, p. 207** *Possible revision:*

In general, pop culture enthusiasts define *cosplay* as an activity in which people wear costumes based on characters from popular culture. These characters come from movies, television shows, comic books, and even video games. The term *cosplay* is a combination of two words: *costume* and *play*. While cosplay might seem like just another form of dressing up, fans consider it a distinct cultural activity, not the same thing as Halloween or a costume party.

Cosplay once appealed to only a tiny segment of the population. Enthusiastic fans of Japanese animation first practiced cosplay in the 1990s. Today, thousands of people do cosplay. Cosplayers aren't just serious anime fans anymore; fans cosplay all different kinds of characters, and all levels of fans attend events in costume, from the casual to the obsessed. Fan conventions are now a huge business. Cosplayers and non-cosplayers alike widely attend events like Comic-Con in San Diego and New York, Dragon Con in Atlanta, and Anime Vegas in Las Vegas. Some pop culture enthusiasts attribute the rise in cosplayers to the popularity of other formerly "nerdy" things. Almost everyone loves comic book movies and shows like the Marvel Cinematic Universe, fantasy series like *Game of Thrones* and *Harry Potter*, and sci-fi movies like the *Star Wars* series.

**Exercise 22-a, p. 209** *Possible revisions:*

1. Dr. Sanchez taught me to write more clearly, to avoid grammatical errors, and to be punctual.
2. A good story requires both an introduction that grabs readers' attention and a satisfying conclusion.
3. I would rather you ask for directions than get lost.
4. Tiana had to feed the cat, water the plants, and give the pet sitter a house key.
5. Hedy Lamar was not only an actress, but also an inventor who helped to create the technology that led to Wi-Fi and Bluetooth.

**Exercise 22-b, p. 210**

1. a; 2. b; 3. a; 4. c; 5. c

**Exercise 22-c, p. 212** *Possible revision:*

We all go to college for different reasons: to get an education, to meet new people, and to gain the skills for a job. The best programs reach several of these goals at the same time. I like to take courses that both interest me and build skills that will lead to a job. It is great to learn about something in class and then apply it in a practical situation. Wanting to apply what I learn is why I am doing an internship. I have the opportunity to gain credits, professional skills, and important contacts all at the same time. I feel safer starting my career early than waiting until after graduation.

I am a computer science major, so I am interning at a tech company. At first, my internship duties were just the basics: making copies, answering the phone, and filing some papers. However, I would often either shadow my supervisor as she attended meetings or assist her in higher-level duties. As time went on, she taught me how to use the company's systems, how she accomplished her daily tasks, and how to do basic coding. After a few weeks, I was both taking on more exciting projects and learning new skills.

**Exercise 23-a, p. 213**

1. b; 2. b; 3. a; 4. b; 5. b

**Exercise 23-b, p. 215** *Possible revisions:*

1. Adding just one or two sentences to the report will add much more detail.
2. The story goes that H. J. Heinz started out selling homemade horseradish at people's doorsteps.
3. After the host acted so rudely, we left the party disgusted by his immature behavior.
4. Usually, you have to make an account before you can post a comment to an online forum.
5. While Carlos was riding a bike to school, a car almost hit him.

**Exercise 23-c, p. 216** *Possible revision:*

While Jenna was studying for her final, fatigue set in. Jenna had only one exam left, but it was for her least favorite course: economics. She had been surprised to discover how much she struggled in this class. The problem might have been overconfidence. Since Jenna had done well in previous business-related courses, economics had seemed familiar and manageable at first. After a few weeks, she discovered that economics did not overlap with other business courses as much as she'd thought. Studying for the final, she had reached the point where she was just rereading notes and textbooks without understanding the material. A walk to the coffee shop seemed like a good idea.

When Jenna arrived, the coffee shop was quiet. Jenna got a latte. Tasting warm and sweet, the latte was delicious. She spread out her notes and textbooks on the table and started to read again. The change in environment seemed to help. Sixty minutes passed before

Jenna knew it. She felt as if she'd gotten more studying done in that one hour at the coffee shop than in the previous five hours.

**Exercise 24-a, p. 217** *Possible revisions:*

1. My professor asked us to read stories by Flannery O'Connor, an author from the South.
2. I want fruit, but the refrigerator is full of vegetables.
3. Even though Theodore Roosevelt was a popular leader and politician, his true passions were nature and the wilderness.
4. Although New York is his true home, Xavier was born in California.
5. She worked at the library during the day and attended courses in the evenings.

**Exercise 24-b, p. 218** *Possible revisions:*

1. a. While Florence Nightingale was a famous nurse, she was also a writer and a social reformer.
   b. Writer and social reformer Florence Nightingale was a famous nurse.
2. a. Tenskwatawa, an important Native American leader, encouraged his people to give up alcohol along with European clothing and tools.
   b. Important Native American leader Tenskwatawa encouraged his people to give up alcohol, European clothing, and European tools.
3. a. My mother, who is a smart shopper, managed to find the shoes she wanted at a lower price at a different store even though the sale had ended.
   b. Even though the sale had ended, my mother managed to find the shoes she wanted at a lower price at a different store; she's a smart shopper.
4. a. While Graham was fixing his bike this morning, Betty was washing her car.
   b. This morning, Graham was fixing his bike and Betty was washing her car.
5. a. Known for their beautiful landscapes, the Rhone River and the Rhine River both rise out of the Alps of Switzerland.
   b. The Rhone River and the Rhine River, both known for their beautiful landscapes, rise out of the Alps of Switzerland.

**Exercise 24-c, p. 219** *Possible revision:*

Discovered in 1801, the first minor planet was called Ceres. A minor planet orbits a sun, but is neither a planet nor a comet. Over 600,000 minor planets have been registered since then. The Minor Planet Center in Northeastern America handles hundreds of requests each year to officially recognize and name celestial objects.

Although the names used to come primarily from Greek and Roman mythology (such as the minor planet Hermes), popular music often provides a source of naming now. Five objects are named after the 1960s band the Beatles. There is a minor planet Beatles named after the whole band and a minor planet named after each group member. The band's drummer Ringo Starr has the minor planet Starr named after him, even though it isn't a star; it's just a minor planet about five miles in diameter. Other minor planets are named after bands such as Yes and ZZ Top, so maybe one day there will be a minor planet named Lady Gaga.

**Exercise 25-a, p. 221** *Possible revisions:*

1. Because the Red Delicious apple variety stayed ripe for a long time, growers loved it.
2. Growers kept changing the Red Delicious variety over the years. They made the apples redder and even more long-lasting.
3. Unfortunately, there was a negative side effect to their changes. Specifically, the apples tasted worse.
4. Apple researchers in Japan developed the Fuji apple using our old friend the Red Delicious.
5. The researchers who developed the apple gave it the name *Fuji* after the name of their research station.

**Exercise 25-b, p. 223**

1. b; 2. a; 3. a; 4. b; 5. a

**Exercise 25-c, p. 224** *Possible revision:*

Key West is the southernmost city in the continental United States, just barely above the Tropic of Cancer. In fact, Key West is nearly as far south as Hawaii, a fact that surprises many people. It is interesting to see how alike and unlike Key West and Hawaii are. Although they are so close, they are quite different physically. Key West is a string of coral islands lying in a shallow coral sea. Hawaii, on the other hand, is a set of separate islands perched on the tops of gigantic volcanic mountains, rising abruptly out of very deep water. Key West is surrounded by other islands and is only a short distance from the Florida mainland, a mere seventy miles. Cuba is close by too, only ninety miles south of Key West. Hawaii, by comparison, is one of the most physically isolated places in the entire world. The native plants and animals in Key West and Hawaii are very different, too. Virtually every plant and animal in Key West is also found everywhere else in the Caribbean. Hawaii's isolation meant that the original stock of plants and animals was extremely limited. The few things that did get to Hawaii diversified and specialized in amazing ways since they had so little competition from other species. As a result, many plants and animals in Hawaii are found nowhere else in the world.

**Exercise 26-a, p. 225** *Possible revisions:*

1. a. She had to stay up late last night, so this morning she is sleeping in.
   b. Because she had to stay up late last night, this morning she is sleeping in.
2. a. Trying to sell a house in this economic climate is tough. Nobody can get a loan.
   b. Trying to sell a house in this economic climate is tough because nobody can get a loan.
3. a. Elizabeth Cochrane Seaman was a pioneering investigative reporter; she was better known by her pen name Nellie Bly.
   b. Elizabeth Cochrane Seaman was a pioneering investigative reporter, although she was better known by her pen name Nellie Bly.
4. a. He had two competing desires: He wanted to make it to class on time, but he wanted to go back to sleep.
   b. He had two competing desires. He wanted to make it to class on time, but he wanted to go back to sleep.
5. a. Cheetahs are one of the lightest big cat species; they are also the fastest.
   b. Cheetahs are one of the lightest big cat species, and they are also the fastest.

**Exercise 26-b, p. 227** *Possible revisions:*

1. Correct
2. What's wrong with the car? It keeps making a grinding noise.
3. W.E.B. Du Bois led the Niagara Movement, which was a civil rights group founded in 1905.
4. Correct
5. Hilda Solis was a congresswoman, but she later became the Secretary of Labor.

**Exercise 26-c, p. 228** *Possible revision:*

Parking at the school has always been difficult, but it seems to be getting worse every year. Although there are always more students, there is never any more parking. Like a lot of urban schools, the campus is relatively small in proportion to the number of students. This naturally causes a lot of problems for parking. To begin with, full-time staff and faculty get half of the existing parking; the other half is for two-hour parking meters, which are always full. There is actually a fair amount of street parking near the campus. The problem is that it is first come, first served. If you have afternoon labs or a late meeting, all the spaces are long gone by the time you get to school. There is no way to tell how much time it will take to find a parking place: It could be a few minutes or a half hour. Fortunately, the campus is in a good neighborhood. Students and faculty do not have to worry about safety when walking to their cars, even after dark. The one bit of good news is that the school is in the process of buying a large vacant parking lot a couple of miles from campus. The school will then charter some buses so that it can run a continuous shuttle from the parking lot to campus. This change can't come soon enough.

**Exercise 27-a, p. 229**

1. The integration of so many different ideas takes a lot of time and effort.
2. The ranking of all the qualifying teams is always controversial.
3. Examination of the documents clearly shows that the defendant is innocent. [OK]
4. Everyone on the team is worried about losing the game. [OK]
5. One of the trees in our neighborhood has crashed down onto the power line.

**Exercise 27-b, p. 230**

1. During the summer, the thunder and the lightning in our area are just amazing.
2. The light in the garage and the light over the sink need replacing.
3. What "football" means in America and what it means in the rest of the world are totally different things. [OK]
4. Loud drums, thunderclaps, and even our doorbell frighten my little sister.
5. The characters and the plot of his latest book are just like those in all his other books.

**Exercise 27-c, p. 231**

All products containing chocolate in any form come from the seeds of the cacao tree. The Mayas in Central America were the first to discover how to produce chocolate from cacao seeds. A number of large, melon-shaped pods grow directly on the trunk and larger branches of the cacao tree. Each of these pods contains up to forty almond-shaped seeds. The seeds, after being removed from the pod, fermented, and dried, are transformed into the commercial cocoa bean.

The first step in producing chocolate from the cacao beans is to remove the outer shells. What remains after the shells have been removed are called nibs. Nibs contain a high percentage of a natural fat called cocoa butter. When heated and ground, the nibs release cocoa butter. The mixture of cocoa butter and finely ground nibs forms a liquid called chocolate liquor. The chocolate liquor, after being cooled and molded into little cakes, is what we know as baking chocolate. Baking chocolate and sugar are at the heart of all those wonderful chocolate goodies that almost everyone loves.

**Exercise 28-a, page 233** *Possible revisions:*

1. We did not hear about the proposal, so we need to talk about the details.
2. The street is full of striking employees who are protesting low pay and poor benefits.
3. The coast suffered a lot of damage because the weather forecast did not predict the storm.
4. The fact that the governor and the legislature are virtually at war with each other has brought the state to its knees.
5. San Francisco is one of the most photographed cities in the world. This fame makes the city a natural tourist destination.

**Exercise 28-b, page 234** *Possible revisions:*

1. Correct
2. All of the candidates who were in the running were shocked by the results, even the candidate who won.
3. My roommate met an old friend recently. Her friend is going to law school now.
4. Besides bringing a shovel, Dalit brought food for us to eat on our camping trip. We might

not need the shovel, but the food will come in handy.

5. In his speech, Louis argued that the best way to increase involvement in student government is to give a tuition break to members of the student senate. The speech happened last week.

**Exercise 28-c, page 235** *Possible revision:*

"Star Wars" was the nickname of a US military program. The name came from the popular sci-fi film series. "Star Wars" was a large research program designed to provide military defense in outer space. The program was initiated in the 1980s by the president, who was Ronald Reagan at the time. The 1980s was the height of the cold war. The national defense strategy at the time was "mutually assured destruction." The term basically means that when two sides have nuclear weapons, they both won't use them. The president thought this strategy wouldn't work and wanted a better defense system.

Although the system had the official title of "Strategic Defense Initiative," the public never embraced the official title as much as the catchier title "Star Wars." The name was initially an insult from Senator Ted Kennedy meant to make fun of the initiative. However, the name stuck. The Department of Defense researched and developed "Star Wars" throughout the 1980s. The project was heavily funded for years. However, "Star Wars" underwent major cutbacks once the cold war ended. The project ended officially in 1993.

**Exercise 29-a, page 237**

1. Our cousins visit San Juan often; last year we and they made the trip together.
2. The two most vocal women, Shandra and I, were asked to petition the mayor.
3. In the review session, the TA did a sample problem for my lab partner and me.
4. The other interns and I gave a presentation at the planning meeting.
5. The problem is the government's characterizing immigrants as criminals.

**Exercise 29-b, page 238**

1. She and her little dog returned to Kansas.
2. It was they, not the mayor, who finally raised the money to repair the bridge.
3. Correct
4. Did he ever figure out what they should have said to her?
5. They ordered it especially for my mother and me.

**Exercise 29-c, page 239**

When I was in high school, my father and I would build a new house every other summer. My father and mother were teachers, so he and she always had summers off. During the first summer, my father and I would pour the foundation and do the framing and roofing. During the school year, a general contractor would supervise the plumbing, wiring, and other specialties. The following summer, my father and I [OK] would finish the interior work. During the next school year, my mother would take charge of all the interior decoration, and then she would put the house on the market.

When you build a house, much of the work is actually done by specialized subcontractors: plumbers, electricians, plasterers, woodworkers, tilers, and so on. Convenience is part of the reason we work with our general contractor, Richard. It is he who hires specialists for each house. He works with many subcontractors, so he [OK] knows which of them are available, do the best work, and have the experience. My father and I [OK] can focus on the building and rely on him to find the specialists.

**Exercise 30-a, page 241**

1. I left my towel in the locker that is nearest the door.
2. The fact that Hawaii does not go on daylight saving time always confuses people.

3. I usually check [OK] my e-mail as soon as I get back from lunch.
4. Yesterday he deposited the money in an account that he keeps [OK] at the local credit union.
5. The accident occurred on a stretch of road that has a reputation for being dangerous.

**Exercise 30-b, page 242**

1. b; 2. c; 3. a; 4. c; 5. a

**Exercise 30-c, page 244**

Provence is a region in the southeast corner of France, which borders Italy. The name Provence refers to the fact that it was the first province created by the ancient Romans outside the Italian peninsula. Today, Provence still contains an amazing number of well-preserved Roman ruins. The beautiful beach and Mediterranean Sea run along the region. The largest and best-known city in Provence is Marseille. The ancient Greeks and Romans called it Massalia, and used it as an important port and trading post. Now, Marseille remains a center of commerce for France and all of Europe. While a few other big towns exist on the coast, Provence is still famous for its wild country and beautiful scenery. Provence is especially known for its abundance of wildflowers in the spring. These flowers are used to make some of the world's most expensive perfumes.

**Exercise 31-a, page 245**

1. a; 2. a; 3. the; 4. the; 5. an

**Exercise 31-b, page 246**

1. There was confusion about the instructions.
2. Correct
3. Most countries tax cigarettes and alcohol heavily.
4. We don't have the training we need to fix the computer.
5. Most of the nonprofit organizations I know are dedicated to a great cause.

**Exercise 31-c, page 247**

When I was a young child, sports were only available through schools. That meant that during the summer, children had no access to organized sports when they actually had free time to do them. The situation is different for children today. A big problem for them is having so many options that they don't know what to pick. Should children play Little League baseball, should they do tennis at Parks and Recreation, or should they take swimming lessons at the YMCA? Should they take karate, or should they take tae kwon do? It sometimes seems that children today are lost in a sea of options, making it easy to flit from a sport to another without getting very good at one of them. Maybe it is not so critical with individual sports or martial arts because they can be started up again without too much loss of skills. On a sports team it is a totally different matter because it takes a long time to build team spirit or teamwork.

**Exercise 32-a, page 249**

1. Pulitzer Prize winner Toni Morrison, who passed away in 2019, wrote about important themes like the African American experience and female identity.
2. Most people are terrified of being bitten by a shark, yet far more people are injured each year by dogs than sharks.
3. Bahir is dropping by my apartment later, so I suppose I should pick up my dirty clothes and wash the dishes.
4. Correct
5. On my birthday, I am going to see my favorite singer, Elton John.

**Exercise 32-b, page 251**

1. To keep people from sneaking up on him, folk hero Wild Bill Hickok placed crumpled newspapers around his bed.
2. Correct
3. Although Wally Amos is best known for his brand of cookies, he was also the first African

American talent agent for the William Morris Agency.
4. Someone called for you this morning and left a strange message.
5. Correct

**Exercise 32-c, page 252**

The first true clocks were built in the thirteenth century, an era when accurate timekeeping became increasingly important. There were some existing timekeeping devices, such as sundials. However, these were often used in situations that were not ideal. Sundials were useless at night when there was insufficient light for casting a shadow. The wind could blow out candles, which also could be used to estimate the time. The timekeeping devices that used streams could freeze in winter. By the thirteenth century, the European monastery was a major social organization that depended on precise, accurate, and reliable timing. The monks' cooperative work efforts required them to coordinate their duties in terms of timing. This was an important need that called for a machine that could keep reliable time. Because of this, the modern clock was devised.

**Exercise 33-a, page 253**

1. I have three essays to complete for my women's studies class.
2. Alfred Wegner's degrees were in astronomy, but his life's work was in meteorology.
3. A starfish's eyes are located at the tips of each of its arms.
4. Hold the acid at arm's length and make sure you're wearing your safety goggles.
5. Sheila wasn't aware that her parents' new house was so big.

**Exercise 33-b, page 254**

1. Here's a fun fact: the saxophone's inventor was named Adolphe Sax.
2. If we aren't out the door in five minutes, we're going to be late for the Johnsons' anniversary party.
3. Correct
4. I'm not a fan of coffee, but you're welcome to have as many cups as you want.
5. It isn't Florida's high temperature that's so suffocating; it's its humidity.

**Exercise 33-c, page 255**

The word *parasite* comes from a Greek word meaning a person who doesn't do honest work but depends entirely on wealthy and powerful patrons' handouts. Biologists adopted the term to describe a huge variety of creatures that steal their nourishment from hosts, often causing their host's death. For many animals, it's just the way they have to survive. However, the behavior of parasites strikes most humans as vicious and ugly. It isn't a surprise that their behavior has captured many writers' and filmmakers' imaginations.

One of the best fictional depictions of parasites is in the science fiction movie *Alien*. In that movie, a spaceship's crew discovers small aliens that attack someone's neck. Later, a creature pierces through the man's stomach and leaps out. The alien laid an egg in his abdomen; the eggs hatched and chewed through his intestines. This horrible scenario is actually based on the real behavior of parasitic wasps. They lay their eggs in living caterpillars. As the eggs mature, they eat the internal organs of the caterpillar, sparing only the organs necessary to keep the caterpillar alive. When the eggs are fully mature, they erupt through the caterpillar's skin, leaving behind their hollowed-out host's body.

**Exercise 34-a, page 257**

1. Gage asked, "When can we eat?"
2. "The store opens at ten," she said, "but the deli won't open until eleven."
3. "Mary Shelley wrote, 'Nothing is so painful to the human mind as a great and sudden change,'" the speaker told the lecture attendees.

4. “Watch out for that tree!” the lumberjack shouted.
5. I have a hard time understanding the plot of the story “An Occurrence at Owl Creek Bridge,” yet my essay on it is due soon.

**Exercise 34-b, page 258**

1. The British singer Adele said that one of her favorite songs to perform was “Rolling in the Deep.”
2. When describing the song, she said, “it’s a dark bluesy gospel disco tune.”
3. Are you still writing a paper about Langston Hughes’s poem “I, Too, Sing America”?
4. Correct
5. The sign read “Keep Out,” but I asked myself, “Who would mind if I went in?”

**Exercise 34-c, page 259**

Literary works have long served as a basis for lyrics used in popular music, including classic rock hits such as Led Zeppelin’s “Ramble On.” That song makes references to Tolkien’s *Lord of the Rings*. One line mentions the “darkest depths of Mordor,” and another refers to an evil being named “Gollum.” Have you seen the music video for the country song “If I Die Young”? It shows a member of The Band Perry holding a book containing Alfred, Lord Tennyson’s poem “The Lady of Shalott,” which influenced the song’s story. “Sink me in the river at dawn,” the vocalist sings, “send me away with the words of a love song.” This is a reference to the ending of the poem. A tune by the Indigo Girls, “Left Me a Fool,” refers to the same poem. They even mention it by name, singing, “You remind me of Shalott / Only made of shadows even though you’re not.”

Lana Del Rey, who has won many musical awards, mentions Nabokov’s novel *Lolita* in “Off to the Races”; at one point she sings, “I said, ‘Hon’ you never looked so beautiful / As you do now my man.’” Several of her other songs make references to poets Walt Whitman and Allen Ginsberg. Even heavy metal bands have gotten into the act. For instance, the band Avenged Sevenfold took its name from the famous biblical story of Cain and Abel. The fourth chapter of the book of Genesis indicates Cain’s death would be “avenged sevenfold.”

# Bibliography


## Chapter 3

Chandler Project. August 11, 2008, Chandlerproject.org.

Edberg, Henrik. "Why You Should Write Things Down." *The Positivity Blog*, September 12, 2007, www.positivityblog.com/index.php/2007/09/12/why-you-should-write-things-down/.

Gardner, John N., and Betsy O. Barefoot. "Managing Your Time." *Your College Experience: Strategies for Success*, 10th ed., Bedford/St. Martin's, 2012.

## Chapter 4

Feldman, Robert. *The Liar in Your Life: The Way to Truthful Relationships*. Hachette Book Group, 2009, pp. 59–60.

Fishman, Rob. "Beating Cheating." *The Cornell Daily*, November 8, 2006, cornellsun.com/node/19684.

Fleming, Grace. "Cheating: Why It's Different in College." *About.com: Homework/Study Tips*, homeworktips.about.com/od/homeworkhelp/a/collegecheating.htm.

Gabriel, Trip. "Plagiarism Lines Blur for Students in Digital Age." *The New York Times*, August 1, 2010, www.nytimes.com/2010/08/02/education/02cheat.html.

## Chapter 5

Burgess, Heidi. "I-Messages and You-Messages." Beyondintractability.org, October 2003, www.beyondintractability.org/essay/I-messages/.

Martin, Judith. Miss Manners' Guide to Rearing Perfect Children. Penguin Books, 1985.

Schiller, Emily. "Taking Advantage of Office Hours." Backtocollege.com, www.back2college.com/officehours.htm.

Stafford, Diane. "Study Finds That Happy Workers Are More Productive Workers." TampaBay.com, April 10, 2009, www.tampabay.com/news/business/workinglife/article990727.ece.